CITYSPOTS
PALE[RMO]

Fran Folsom

Written by Fran Folsom
Updated by Petulia Melideo

Published by Thomas Cook Publishing
A division of Thomas Cook Tour Operations Limited
Company registration No: 1450464 England
The Thomas Cook Business Park, 9 Coningsby Road
Peterborough PE3 8SB, United Kingdom
Email: books@thomascook.com, Tel: +44 (0)1733 416477
www.thomascookpublishing.com

Produced by The Content Works Ltd
Aston Court, Kingsmead Business Park, Frederick Place
High Wycombe, Bucks HP11 1LA
www.thecontentworks.com

Series design based on an original concept by Studio 183 Limited

ISBN: 978-1-84157- 940-5

First edition © 2006 Thomas Cook Publishing
This second edition © 2008 Thomas Cook Publishing
Text © Thomas Cook Publishing
Maps © Thomas Cook Publishing/PCGraphics (UK) Limited

Series Editor: Kelly Anne Pipes
Project Editor: Linda Bass
Production/DTP: Steven Collins

Printed and bound in Spain by GraphyCems

Cover photography (Palermo Cathedral) © Jean Pierre/World Pictures/Photoshot

All rights reserved. No part of this publication may be reproduced, stored in a retrieval system or transmitted, in any form or any means, electronic, mechanical, recording or otherwise, in any part of the world, without prior permission of the publisher. Requests for permission should be made to the publisher at the above address.

Although every care has been taken in compiling this publication, and the contents are believed to be correct at the time of printing, Thomas Cook Tour Operations Limited cannot accept any responsibility for errors or omission, however caused, or for changes in details given in the guidebook, or for the consequences of any reliance on the information provided. Descriptions and assessments are based on the author's views and experiences when writing and do not necessarily represent those of Thomas Cook Tour Operations Limited.

CONTENTS

INTRODUCING PALERMO
Introduction 6
When to go 8
The Mafia 12
History 14
Lifestyle 16
Culture 18

MAKING THE MOST OF PALERMO
Shopping 22
Eating & drinking 26
Entertainment & nightlife 30
Sport & relaxation 32
Accommodation 34
The best of Palermo 40
Suggested itineraries 42
Something for nothing 44
When it rains 46
On arrival 48

THE CITY OF PALERMO
Quattro Canti &
  the Albergheria 60
Via Roma & the Vucciria 80
La Kalsa –
  the Historic Quarter 96

OUT OF TOWN TRIPS
Mondello 110
Monreale 116
Trapani & Marsala 124

PRACTICAL INFORMATION
Directory 142
Emergencies 154

INDEX 156

MAPS
Palermo 52
Quattro Canti &
  the Albergheria 61
Via Roma & the Vucciria 81
La Kalsa –
  the Historic Quarter 97
Around Palermo 112

CITYSPOTS

SYMBOLS KEY

The following symbols are used throughout this book:

⓪ address ⓣ telephone ⓕ fax ⓦ website address ⓔ email
⓪ opening times ⓝ public transport connections ⓘ important

The following symbols are used on the maps:

- ℹ️ information office
- ✈️ airport
- ➕ hospital
- 🛡️ police station
- 🚌 bus station
- 🚆 railway station
- ✝️ cathedral
- ❶ numbers denote featured cafés & restaurants
- ◼ points of interest
- ⭕ city
- ○ large town
- ○ small town
- = motorway
- — main road
- — minor road
- — railway

Hotels and restaurants are graded by approximate price as follows:
£ budget price **££** mid-range price **£££** expensive **£££+** very expensive

◗ *Of all Palermo's ecclesiastical buildings, the Cattedrale is the most imposing*

INTRODUCING
Palermo

INTRODUCING PALERMO

Introduction

There is an Italian saying that 'the mystique of Palermo lingers with you forever'. In a gorgeous bay underneath the hulking Monte Pellegrino and fronting the wide and fertile Conca d'Oro (Golden Shell) valley, Palermo is magnificently sited.

This is a city of multi-layered history, starting with its founding as a Phoenician colony. It was taken by the Carthaginians in the 5th century, then came the Greeks, and in 254 BC it was conquered by the Romans. Palermo's most glorious time came in AD 831 when it was captured by the Arabs, under whose rule it blossomed as an Islamic cultural and intellectual centre. Two centuries later, under the Normans, Palermo was Europe's greatest metropolis.

By way of contrast, the 20th century was one of social and economic decline for the city. Allied bombs during World War II destroyed much of the port area and over seventy of the city's historic churches. Today major restorations are ongoing at a painstakingly slow pace.

There is no other city in Italy quite like Palermo. On the cusp of a new beginning, it also celebrates its diverse history. Visiting here is thrilling for what the city has to offer, but it can also be a challenge. Traffic is horrible as cars, trucks and buses clog the narrow streets, often coming to a complete standstill for hours. This has caused a yellow cloud of pollution to hang constantly over the city making air quality less than desirable, covering cars and buildings with dust.

In the year 2000 Palermo's Via Roma registered a higher level of air pollution than any other main street in Italy. City officials are working to put restrictions into place that will allow driving into Palermo only on certain days of the week. This is a city best seen on foot or by bicycle. Be careful, traffic not withstanding, Palermitans

INTRODUCTION

drive fast and stop for nothing that gets in their way. The sort of manoeuvre that would attract outrage on the roads at home might well gain admiring applause here.

You won't see beggars or homeless people in the streets. What is commonplace here is petty crime – you would be well advised to avoid the markets and back street areas after dark, and don't flash around large amounts of money. This form of social menace is a throwback to the days when the Mafia used the city as its power base and created an atmosphere of ad hoc lawlessness. That has largely gone underground now, but the alternative (if undesirable) systems of thought and social organisation that the Mafia represented somehow only add to Palermo's compelling air of intrigue.

Most areas are safe in the daytime and nothing should stop you from enjoying the city. Vestiges from the 9th to the 12th century are abundant. But, it's the re-creation of the city between the 16th and 17th centuries that gave Palermo the appearance it has today: a straightforward grid pattern, jumbled by the prior existence of an Eastern beginning, and the destruction from World War II bombs.

Palermo's churches have always been richly endowed, either by wealthy families or monastic orders, and so visitors flock to them; from the Cattedrale to the richly coloured mosaics of Cappella Palatina inside the Royal Apartments, to the Norman built La Martorana. Along with these are many fine examples of baroque architecture such as San Giuseppe dei Teatini and Santa Caterina. As well as being interesting from an architectural point of view, Palermo also boasts three excellent museums, the festivals and marketplaces, the puppet theatre and a plethora of outstanding restaurants.

Despite all this, Palermo is a jewel of the Mediterranean. No visit to Sicily would be complete without a stop in Palermo, where you will come not just to know the island, but to understand it.

INTRODUCING PALERMO

When to go

Palermo is perennially gorgeous, though it's at its balmiest between April and October. If you're uncomfortable in very hot weather, it might be an idea to avoid July and August. Winter tends to be a touch chilly, which makes a fine excuse for cosying up in one of the local restaurants, where you can take advantage of the cold weather with a thoroughly warming menu. If possible, visit the city during main religious holidays, especially Holy Week (see page 10). This way you will experience the real charm of the city in full festival mode.

SEASONS & CLIMATE

The best months for warm (but not hot) weather are May, June and September, with October and November pleasant for hiking and swimming. Summer brings blistering heat blown in by the sirocco wind from North Africa. This season also brings thousands of visitors, limited hotel availability in the resort areas such as Mondello, and higher prices. During December and January Palermo is damp, cold and rainy, making a heavy coat and umbrella necessary. Spring arrives early, in February, when the almond trees blossom.

ANNUAL EVENTS
January
Orthodox Epiphany (6 Jan) Procession at Piana degli Albanesi, traditional costumes and the passing out of oranges.

February
Baroque Carnival Centuries ago the aristocracy of Palermo would show off their wealth with lavish masked balls and parades

WHEN TO GO

◮ *Christmas lights in the streets of Palermo*

throughout the city. Today the pre-Lent carnival is a citywide celebration of Palermo and its history. For a schedule of events, contact the tourist office. (☏ (091) 605 8351)

INTRODUCING PALERMO

March & April
Easter (Begins 5 Apr 2009; 28 Mar 2010) Holy Week is celebrated with religious processions highlighting the last days of Christ's life. The Cocchieri (coachmen) procession on Good Friday has costumed participants carrying the statues of the Madonna and Christ all over the city. The Good Friday Procession dei Misteri in Monreale (see page 116), where townspeople dress in traditional costume, is not to be missed. Brotherhoods of men, wearing blue satin hoods over their faces, carry crosses and the statue of the Madonna from the Duomo throughout the hilly streets of the village.

April
St George's Day (23 Apr) St George is celebrated with a procession at Piana degli Albanesi.

June–Sept
KalsArt Festival A summer-long festival of live music, theatre and cinema events in the La Kalsa district Ⓦ www.kalsart.it

July
Festino di Santa Rosalia (Festival of St Rosalia) (Begins 15 July) Commemorates the patron saint of Palermo, who saved the city from the plague. Six days of processions and celebrations end with fireworks over the harbour.

August
Feast of the Assumption (15 Aug) An island-wide celebration, capped off with fireworks.
Il Palio dei Normanni (12–14 Aug) Medieval pageants and jousting contests in Piazza Armerina. Ⓦ www.paliodeinormanni.com

September
Pilgrimage to Monte Pellegrino (4 Sept) This time, a pilgrimage to honour Saint Rosalia.

September–December
Settimana de Musica Sacra (Festival of Sacred Music) At weekends in Monreale's churches (see page 123).

November
Festival of the Dead (2 Nov) Halloween-style celebrations, as deceased relatives are believed to return and leave gifts for children.

December
Feast of the Immaculate Conception (8 Dec) A holy day when statues of Mary are honoured around the city.

PUBLIC HOLIDAYS
New Year's Day 1 Jan
Epiphany 6 Jan
Easter Sunday 12 Apr 2009; 4 Apr 2010
Easter Monday 13 Apr 2009, 5 Apr 2010
Liberation Day 25 Apr
Labour Day 1 May
Feast of St Rosalia 15 July
Feast of the Assumption 15 Aug
Feast of the Immaculate Conception 8 Dec
Christmas Day 25 Dec
St Stephen's Day 26 Dec

INTRODUCING PALERMO

The Mafia

"The Mafia is oppression, arrogance, greed, self-enrichment, power and hegemony above and against all other. It is not an abstract concept, or a state of mind, or a literary term... It is a criminal organization regulated by unwritten but iron and inexorable rules... The myth of a courageous and generous 'man of honor' must be destroyed, because a Mafioso is just the opposite.'

Cesare Terranova, Italian Magistrate, murdered in 1979

Palermo's wealth of culture – and that of Sicily in general – has been overshadowed by the region's history with the mob. News media and the entertainment industry have sometimes tried – occasionally successfully – to portray the Sicilian Mafia's activities as a worldwide metaphor for violence and organised crime. Mario Puzo's novel *The Godfather* rocked the country and was later adapted into an Academy Award-winning film that became the first part of a trilogy.

The Mafia (or Cosa Nostra) today is a symptom of the country's endemic political corruption, a phenomenon which has only worsened. In recent years it has been openly acknowledged that a large part of the funds pouring into Sicily from Rome and the European Union, ostensibly to redevelop and restore Palermo's city centre and other areas of Sicily, are unaccounted for, channelled to dubious businessmen, or simply gone into the coffers of noted Mafia leaders.

The subtle control exerted by the Mafia is typically hidden, but occasionally it does erupt in the news. In more recent times Mafia issues have maintained a high profile, following the instigation of the struggle to reassert the state's authority in the wake of a number of assassinations of anti-Mafia crusaders: in the early 1990s, two of Palermo's leading anti-Mafia judges, Giovanni Falcone and Paolo

THE MAFIA

Borsellino, were assassinated (as were members of their families) within the space of a few weeks. Since then, the arrest of leading Mafia figures, starting with the arrest of the *capo dei capi* (boss of bosses) Salvatore Raiina in 1993, has seen the tide turning against the Cosa Nostra, helped by the testimony of many informers.

However, the problem is deeply rooted and unlikely to disappear completely, despite the efforts of various individuals. The leader among these is Leoluca Orlando, mayor of Palermo from 1993 to 2001, whose policy was to fight corruption at the municipal level by removing companies with links to organised crime from the tenders list of new contracts. Despite reversals, including disavowal by his own Christian Democrat party, Orlando has continued his fight at a national level, at the head of his own Rete (National) party. Proof that Palermo is still a key Mafia city came in November 2007, when Salvatore Lo Piccolo, who is suspected of being the latest boss of bosses was arrested when police raided a meeting of Mafia leaders here.

Fortunately, for the casual traveller, the Mafia has little relevance, in fact you'd have to try very hard even to be aware of the organisation's existence; the closest you will get to it is through the headlines in the local newspapers. Having said that, it is the ridiculously romanticised cinematic portrayal of the Cosa Nostra in *The Godfather* trilogy that actually draws some travellers to Sicily in the hope of visiting locations that appear in the films. Most of the action that was actually shot on the island was done so in towns and villages away from Palermo itself, although the climactic scenes of *The Godfather Part III* were filmed outside the city's Teatro Massimo (see page 74).

You can easily avoid contact with the mob during your stay in the city: just take sensible precautions and you will avoid having your valuables snatched by Vespa-borne delinquents, some of whom are destined to be sucked into the lower ranks of the Mafia clans.

INTRODUCING PALERMO

History

Palermo is a city that has been ruled, settled and developed by several cultures. The first to discover it were the Phoenicians in the 7th century BC. They named it 'Ziz', meaning flower. Then came the Romans, who called it 'Panormus' (large port) because of the town's astonishing location on its own beautiful bay in the shadow of the limestone hulk of Monte Pellegrino. But, it was the Arabs who stamped the town with their art and culture when they conquered it in the 9th century, making it the Islamic centre of the Western world.

Under Arabic rule the town expanded beyond the old city centre of Cassaro (from the Arabic Quasr meaning castle or fort); on the harbour the castle or Kalsa (from *al Halisah* – the chosen one) flourished and was buttressed, becoming the primary residence of the Emir.

The Normans, led by Count Roger de Hauteville, arrived in 1072. In a non-violent transfer that mixed Muslims and various ethnic groups together, he allowed everyone to carry on as if nothing had changed. This mixture gave Palermo its beautiful Arab-Norman style of architecture. Roger II, son of the Count and later crowned King of Sicily, spared no expense when it came to luxurious things. He built two extravagant palaces – La Zisa (see page 88) and La Cuba – and had formal Oriental gardens created for them. Roger surrounded himself with intellectuals from around the world. This debauchery ended when Frederick II of Swabia took command of Sicily in 1212, restoring the town's markets and harbour, making it a business centre again. The Swabians were ousted by the Angevins, who were conquered by the Spaniards, who were overthrown in turn in the 18th century by the Bourbons of Naples, who decorated Palermo with glorious baroque palaces.

HISTORY

The 19th century brought international trade and commerce, with Palermo outgrowing its boundaries. New streets such as the Via della Libertà, were built and lined with angular-style buildings; this was Palermo's last gasp at being an industrial centre. In the 20th century the bombings of World War II nearly destroyed the historical nucleus of the city, and then came a devastating earthquake in 1968. The medieval quarters went into decline as new, ugly buildings were built in the city's outer areas.

On centuries-old streets you will notice a sense of change and pride in the air. The city, thanks to its former mayor Leoluca Orlando and funds from the European Union, is in the midst of a citywide re-evaluation and restoration programme to develop new uses for its magnificent historical areas and buildings. Diego Cammarata, who was first elected mayor in 2001, secured his re-election in 2007 with a manifesto that promised to modernise the city without compromising its considerable cultural heritage.

In evidence around Palermo is the triskele – *the symbol of Sicily*

INTRODUCING PALERMO

Lifestyle

The Palermo of centuries ago was dignified, its buildings shone with colour and the air was free of pollution from cars, trains and buses. Nowadays the narrow streets are terribly clogged with traffic, pushcarts of foods and wares, and continuous construction making it best to navigate Palermo on foot, or, to reach the outskirts or specific sights, by bus. Even cycling is dangerous, as Sicilians are fast drivers notorious at stopping for nothing that gets in their way.

Palermo is run down, it is noisy, crowded, neglected, and, in some areas, seedy and still bombed out from World War II. This is a city with no place to go but up, one that has re-invented itself many times over and is on the verge of doing so again. There is a lot to see, even if some of the sights are in dire need of repair.

Twenty-first-century Palermitans are showing great pride in their history and culture. Tourism is the main infrastructure and, to the delight of visitors, the city finally has the financial resources to dust off and preserve its beautiful theatres, cathedrals, palaces and museums.

As the capital of Sicily and its largest city, Palermo is a fast, brash and exciting place whose residents work hard and play hard. They have big city ways of dressing, dining, art, theatre, music and nightlife. That said, Palermo boasts a large and visible gay and lesbian community of activists who contribute to the city scene artistically and culturally.

The current historical and cultural rejuvenation has brought along a new way of thinking: live in the moment but preserve the past. Most of Palermo, with its beautiful antique baroque, Byzantine and Moorish architecture might seem like a place suspended in time. But walk one or two blocks in any direction and there is 21st-century architecture, restaurants, cinemas, nightlife and shops.

LIFESTYLE

Like any other big city Palermo has its problems, but, this is a city not to be missed. Walk the streets and alleys, smell the aromas rising up from pushcarts and enjoy the traditional foods, attend cultural performances at theatres and museums, sit in the lush gardens and parks and absorb the sounds of this marvellous place.

⬤ *Street markets are part of the Palermitan way of life*

INTRODUCING PALERMO

Culture

At one time Palermo was the first stop on anyone's Grand Tour. From a cultural standpoint it has been the preferred hangout of writers, artists and poets for centuries. They were drawn here by the erotic beauty and Arabic-influenced mysticism of the city and its surroundings.

Fortunately several nationalities left their indelible mark on Palermo's architecture and cultural scene. The city's museums have been working hard to preserve this history and to educate the masses with exhibits and seminars showing artefacts of the various cultures.

In that vein, the city pursues a cultural programme, 'Palermo Opens its Doors', which takes place every weekend in May. This admirable initiative, in which young people are encouraged to act as tour guides and administrators for various cultural sites and monuments that have long been unable to open due to staff shortages, is already paying off on several levels. Through it, thousands of these youngsters (some of whom are still at school) get to study their city's history and culture and, of course, gain valuable work experience. By working as guides, they propagate the history and points of interest of churches, palaces, villas, works of art, squares and entire quarters of the city. The intrinsic charm of the initiative has done much to stimulate the tourist economy: all funds generated by reopening these venues are ploughed straight back into various cultural restoration schemes. 'Palermo Opens its Doors' was the brainchild of the **Cooperativa Sociale**

▶ *Teatro Politeama Garibaldi reflects the Palmeritan love of performance art*

CULTURE

INTRODUCING PALERMO

Azzurra (W www.coopazzurra.net), an organisation that makes it its business to keep the city's culture alive and well.

Another event, '100 Open Churches' (for information, (091) 740 6035) sees constant success. This excellent initiative's aim is to open 100 abandoned churches and buildings where volunteer guides conduct tours.

Palermitans are mad for live theatre, and, with the restoration of the once-crumbling Teatro Massimo (see page 74) and **Teatro Politeama Garibaldi** (Piazza Ruggero Settimo (091) 605 3315), performances are once again in full swing, with some quite brilliant offerings of jazz, ballet, opera, concerts and classical music. For smaller venues featuring folk music and dance performances, there is **Santa Maria dello Spasimo** (Via dello Spasimo 13 (091) 616 1486) in the La Kalsa area.

In summer an organisation called the **Comune** (W www.comune.palermo.it) puts together open-air events, using local rock bands, which are held in green spaces throughout the city.

The websites W www.palermotourism.com, W www.bestofsicily.com and W www.museidicharme.it feature extensive listings of galleries and theatres and give links to individual sights. Tourist offices stock the free bi-monthly magazine *Agenda*, which lists theatre productions, cultural events and museum times. It can also be found at some hotels.

It's a good idea to check posters placed around the city and in cafés, or the newspapers *Giornale di Sicilia* or *La Gazzetta del Sud*. For sporting events or scores, pick up a copy of either the *Corriere dello Sporto* or the pink newspaper *Gazzetta dello Sporto*.

▶ *The Duomo, a great site to start your visit*

MAKING THE MOST OF
Palermo

MAKING THE MOST OF PALERMO

Shopping

Palermo's shops aren't really concentrated into particular areas or streets (although there are beautiful haute couture establishments all along the elegant Via della Libertà), so you'll have the chance to punish the plastic just about anywhere you go.

SHOPPING

The city is known for its markets. The sprawling market of the Vucciria quarter, between Via Roma and Via Vittorio Emanuele, gives one a good sense of the atmosphere of the city. In a small piazza surrounded by twisting, narrow streets lit by naked light bulbs even

Bustling Vucciria market is typical of Palermo's street-shopping atmosphere

MAKING THE MOST OF PALERMO

on a sunny day, the market holds the true aromas and sights of Palermo: fish stalls overflowing with swordfish heads; huge slabs of tuna hanging on hooks; fresh octopus sitting on blocks of ice; pyramids of blood oranges; rounds of cheeses; ropes of garlic; baskets of red and green peppers; and loaves of fresh baked bread.

Arrive early in the morning to watch the action as customers bargain and haggle with the fishmongers, farmers and bakers. Lunchtime is also a good time for a walk through it as there are several good, inexpensive restaurants, some serving wine right out of the barrel, tucked into the alleys around the marketplace.

◉ *Hand-painted porcelain and ceramics make ideal souvenirs*

SHOPPING

The Borgo Vecchio, between Piazza Sturzo and Piazza Ucciardone, is another noteworthy market. Along with the fish, meats, produce and pastries, are stalls full of colourful jewellery, porcelain, pasta bowls, clothing and leather goods. This is where the younger crowd gathers, as the market stays open late and is in the heart Palermo's nightspots.

USEFUL SHOPPING PHRASES

What time do the shops open/close?
A che ora aprono/chiudono i negozi?
Ah keh ohrah ahprohnoh/kewdohnoh ee nehgotsee?

How much is this?
Quanto costa questo?
Kwantoh kostah kwestoh?

Can I try this on?
Posso provarlo?
Pohsoh prohvarloh?

My size is ...
La mia taglia è ...
Lah meeyah tahlyah eh ...

I'll take this one, thank you
Prenderò questo, grazie
Prehndehroh kwestoh, grahtsyeh

Can you show me the one in the window/this one?
Può mostrarmi quello in vetrina/questo?
Poh mohstrahrmee kwehloh een vehtreenah/kwehstoh?

This is too large/too small/too expensive
Questo è troppo grande/troppo piccolo/troppo caro
Kwestoh eh trohpoh grahndeh/trohpoh peekohloh/trohpoh kahroh

MAKING THE MOST OF PALERMO

Eating & drinking

Agriculture, fishing, cheese making and raising cattle have always played key roles in Sicily's economy. Cheese is big news here. From the making of *cacivallo* (horse cheese) – so called because the rounds of cheeses are left to mature, two by two like horses, linked by a piece of cord straddling a wooden beam – or *pecorino*, a cheese made from ewes' milk, to the renowned ricotta that is used in the preparation of the famed Sicilian crème horns and tutti-frutti, the production of cheese has been a rich traditional process.

At most restaurants you can sample dishes that were invented in Palermo then spread across Sicily. One example is *pasta con le sarde*, a simple dish made with pasta, wild fennel, fresh sardines, anchovies, saffron, sultanas and pine nuts. It is served in both luxurious restaurants and simple family-style *trattorias*.

You can be budget conscious yet still eat well here. Street vendors and small cafés are abundant throughout the city. Another way to cut costs is to shop in the daily markets, where you can create a grand picnic basket of sausages, octopus, olives, salami, fresh fruit and loaves of crusty bread.

In many restaurants the menus are gigantic, offering four courses: *antipasti* (selections of meats and cheeses), *primi* (first

PRICE CATEGORIES
The restaurant price guides used in the book indicate the approximate cost of a three-course meal for one person, excluding drinks, at the time of writing.
£ up to €15   **££** €15–30   **£££** €30–50   **£££+** over €50

EATING & DRINKING

course, usually a pasta or rice dish), *secondi* (second course of fish or meat), and ending with *dolci* (dessert). It is not necessary to order all four; you can select two or even one as long as they are from the two main courses. When it comes to *dolci*, throw your diet to the winds and sample *cassata*, a traditional Sicilian dessert made with fresh ricotta, candied fruit and almonds.

Palermitans enjoy their wine, particularly the sweet, heady wines from Marsala. They like to drink it as an aperitif in the late afternoon, or after dinner with cheese and fruit.

As in other parts of Italy coffee, or espresso, is served strong, dark and almost thick enough to stand a spoon in, and is full of enough caffeine to keep non-Italians awake for three days. True coffee aficionados drink it unsweetened, and without *latte* (milk).

Coffee and wine may be an integral part of the scene in Palermo, but, it is ice cream that Palermitans hold most holy in the food chain. One of the city's glories are its *gelaterie* (ice cream shops). While in Palermo get with the local custom and try a *brioche con gelato* (ice cream in a cinnamon bun) for breakfast – one bite and you'll understand why Palermitans love it so. *Gelaterie* also sell *granita*, made with fruit juice (or syrup) and crushed ice.

Be prepared to dine late. The restaurants that serve lunch do so from 12.30–15.00, then close and don't reopen until 19.30 or later. You will want to make your dinner reservation early in the day as most restaurants are small and book up fast. Weekends are the busiest time, when you need to make your reservations at least three days in advance.

Cafés and *birrerias* are generally open late, while restaurants close their kitchens by midnight. A good thing to remember is that many large restaurants are closed during August, and on Mondays and Tuesdays, several family-owned ones are even closed on Sundays, it is best to call ahead.

/ MAKING THE MOST OF PALERMO

Credit cards are accepted in most of the city's large restaurants, as a rule; cafés and *trattorias* accept only cash, so make sure you've got enough on you at all times. Tips are well received, and if you are obviously a tourist, you can expect to be fawned over in the hope

● *Marzipan galore in Palermo*

EATING & DRINKING

of a sign of your appreciation. There is no set amount: a ten per cent tip is very generous, and something between €2 to €5 is acceptable. For bars, 30 cents is sufficient. Some upmarket restaurants add a service charge (it should be itemised on the bill), and if that is the case no further tip is necessary. By contrast, some of the more old-fashioned, out-of-the-way establishments persist with the *coperto*, a sort of cover charge that's a throwback to the days before mass tourism existed. Just a couple of cents should do very nicely for this.

USEFUL DINING PHRASES

I would like a table for ... people
Vorrei un tavolo per ... persone
Vawrray oon tahvawlaw pehr ... perrsawneh

Waiter/waitress!
Cameriere/cameriera!
Cahmehryereh/cahmehryera!

May I have the bill, please?
Mi dà il conto, per favore?
Mee dah eel cawntaw, pehr fahvohreh?

I am a vegetarian. Does this contain meat?
Sono vegetariano/vegetariana (fem.). Contiene carne?
Sawnaw vejetahreeahnaw/vejetahreeahnah. Contyehneh kahrneh?

MAKING THE MOST OF PALERMO

Entertainment & nightlife

When the sun sets Palermo takes on a different look. The sounds of police sirens permeate the air; streets are empty of pedestrian traffic so it is best to keep to the main thoroughfares. In winter the city centre's bars and *birrerias* tend to close by midnight, but in summer the nightlife continues into the early morning hours.

The area around Via della Libertà has a lively street scene, with cars cruising up and down blasting stereo systems. Bars and clubs come and go, so follow the crowds to the current favourite. Many of the new and trendy clubs are in the northern quarters of the city, particularly around Viale Regione Siciliana. These are upmarket, expensive places to see and be seen in, not really worth the bus or taxi ride to get there.

Via Principe di Belmonte, with its flashy selection of bars and pastry cafés, is a favourite of the young crowd; haunts of students are the bars along the Via dei Candelai (in the Quattro Canti).

Another hot scene for nightlife is the trendy beach resort of Mondello (see page 110), 11 km (7 miles) from the city centre (take buses 806 or 833 from either Piazza Sturzo or Via della Libertà). The last bus returning to Palermo is at 23.00, while a taxi back to the city centre costs €30. Mondello's bars and clubs are the places to see and be seen. On summer nights the bars in the main square are overflowing, spilling out onto the Piazza Mondello, where local youths cruise the strip and open-air discos pulse with music.

Ice cream is a passion in Palermo, and one of the city's nocturnal marvels are its *gelaterie* (ice cream parlours), many of which stay open late, all the better to serve the post-discothèque crowd their *brioche con gelato* (ice cream in a cinnamon bun), usually served

ENTERTAINMENT & NIGHTLIFE

> **WHAT'S ON**
> All of Palermo's tourist offices stock the bi-monthly magazine *Agenda*, which lists theatre times and productions. It's in Italian, but you'll be able to understand what's going on. The following websites feature extensive listings on theatres and cinemas and give links to individual sites:
> Ⓦ www.palermotourism.com
> Ⓦ www.bestofsicily.com

as a breakfast pastry. Some of the best parlours are in the southern part of the city on Corso dei Mille, Via Villareale and at the lower end of Foro Italico.

When it comes to cinema, Hollywood and films have always held a fascination to Palermitans. One of their favourite pastimes is to frequent the many cinemas along Palermo's *cinema via* (movie street), the Via E Amari. Do note that almost all the films on offer will be in Italian, with no original-language subtitles.

A trip to the theatre is ideal if you do speak Italian (or want to learn), especially the alternative smaller live performance theatres whose season runs from November to May. **Teatro Siciliano** (ⓐ Zappala Via Autonomia Siciliana ⓣ (091) 543 380) features productions in Sicilian dialect; **Teatro Biondo** (ⓐ Via Teatro Biondo 11 ⓣ (091) 582 364 Ⓦ www.teatrobiondo.it) also has productions in Sicilian, while **Teatro Libero** (ⓐ Salita Partanna 4, Piazza Marina ⓣ (091) 617 4040 Ⓦ www.teatroliberopalermo.it) specialises in avant-garde productions.

MAKING THE MOST OF PALERMO

Sport & relaxation

SPECTATOR SPORTS
Football
As in all other Italian cities, football is big in Palermo, and the pink and black colours of the local team, **Unione Sportiva Città di Palermo** (w www.ilpalermocalcio.it), are much in evidence. Matches at the Renzo Barbera stadium draw huge and excitable crowds – for event dates, times or scores pick up a copy of the pink newspaper *Gazzetta dello Sporto* or the *Corriere dello Sporto*.

Stadio Comunale Renzo Barbera a Viale del Fante t (091) 690 1211

PARTICIPATION SPORTS
Cycling
If you really want to get your blood pumping and your heart racing, ride a bicycle in Palermo traffic. **Kursaal Kalhesa** (a Foro Umberto 1 t (091) 616 2828) rents bicycles for around €6 per day, while **Toto Cannatella** (a Via Papireto 14a t (091) 322 425) charges €10 per day.

Golf
With the generally mild climate, you can play golf year-round at locations near the city. One course that offers glorious views of mountains and the sea is located in Collesano (40 km/25 miles from Palermo) and is called Le Madonie Golf Club. If you decide to drive there, take the A29 towards Cefalu; buses to Collesano leave from Stazione Centrale. Be sure to check at the station what number bus goes to Collesano as the buses change according to the season.

Le Madonie Golf Club a Via de Bartellucelli, Collesano t (092) 193 4387 w www.lemadoniegolf.com

SPORT & RELAXATION

Tennis

Public tennis courts are located on Viale del Fante, near the northern entrance of Parco della Favorita (bring your own racket). Circolo del Tennis, an institution in Palermo since 1923, has indoor hard surface and outdoor clay courts; rackets can be hired. It is best to call ahead to reserve a court.

Circolo del Tennis ⓐ Viale del Fante 3 ⓘ (091) 544 517
ⓦ www.circolotennis.palermo.it

Watersports

Along with windsurfing, the Albaria Windsurfing Club offers boardsailing, catamarans and sailing on Mondello bay.

Albaria Windsurfing Club ⓐ Viale Regina Elena 89a ⓘ (091) 453 595
ⓦ www.albaria.com

RELAXATION

The best form of exercise while in Palermo is walking. That said, if jogging or running is more to your liking you will not be alone at any of the city's open parks or green spaces: Parco d'Orleans by the University of Palermo, Giardino Inglese on Via della Libertà or the largest park in the city, Parco della Favorita on Via Impertole Federico.

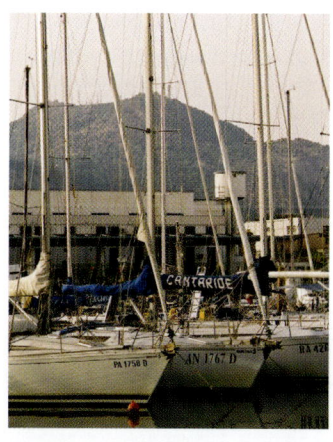

▲ *Yachts in Palermo harbour*

MAKING THE MOST OF PALERMO

Accommodation

July and August, when locals head to the seaside resorts, are considered the low season in the city. With the exception of July, when the festival honouring the city's patron St Rosalia takes place (see page 10), hotel rooms are easy to come by at very good rates. It is still best to reserve as far in advance as possible. The main tourist office on Piazza Castelnuovo (see page 153) can assist with last-minute lodgings.

Hotel prices vary depending on the area of the city that you stay in. Those that are the most reasonably priced can be found on or near the southern ends of Via Maqueda and Via Roma between Stazione Centrale (see page 49) and Via Vittorio Emanuele. In this area the general rule is: the higher the floor the cheaper the price.

In the historical and cultural centres hotels will be more expensive. Most hotels, big or small, include a breakfast of some sort, either coffee and a pastry or a complete hot meal. Fortunately, many of Palermo's hotels are located near public transportation, historical sights or cultural venues.

PRICE CATEGORIES

Hotels conform to a rating system, ranging from 1-star hotels, where rooms may not have private facilities, to 5-star luxury resorts. Breakfast is not usually included in the rates for budget and mid-range hotels. Prices for a single night in a double room for two persons are:

£ up to €65   ££ €65–100   £££ €100–150   £££+ over €150

ACCOMMODATION

HOTELS

B&B Notarbartolo £ Strategically located in the residential district of Palermo, and a few steps away from the Notarbartolo Station, this elegant B&B is a valid alternative to any hotel. ⓐ Via E Notarbartolo 35 ⓣ/ⓕ (091) 730 8333 Ⓝ Bus: 102, 103, 118

Cortese £ There are several advantages to staying here; the terrific price, friendly staff and clean rooms, some overlooking the Ballaro market. ⓐ Via Scarparelli 16 ⓣ/ⓕ (091) 331 722 ⓦ www.hotelcortese.net Ⓝ Bus: 101, 102

Hotel Cavour £ On the fifth floor of a charming old *palazzo*. Rooms are light and airy, and the location is central. ⓐ Via A Manzoni 11 (fifth floor, with a lift) ⓣ/ⓕ (091) 616 2759 ⓦ www.albergocavour.com Ⓝ Bus: 139, 211, 221, 224, 226

Hotel Moderno £ A friendly, family-owned hotel offering small functional rooms. Nothing fancy, but the staff will make you feel very welcome. The third and fourth floors have a lift. ⓐ Via Roma 276 ⓣ/ⓕ (091) 588 683 ⓦ www.hotelmodernopa.com Ⓝ Bus: 101

Orientale £ This hotel has two connections to history: it was once part of the Royal Apartments, and Mussolini stayed here. Rooms are basic but clean. ⓐ Via Maqueda 26 ⓣ (091) 616 5727 ⓕ (091) 616 1193 ⓦ www.albergoorientale.191.it Ⓝ Linea Rossa (red line) bus

Hotel Elite ££ This 18-room hotel is in the heart of Palermo's theatre district. Its small, colourful rooms boast modern frescoes painted by a local artist. ⓐ Via Mariano Stabile 136 ⓣ (091) 329 318 ⓕ (091) 588 614 ⓦ www.hotelelite.info Ⓝ Bus: 101, 102

MAKING THE MOST OF PALERMO

Hotel Excelsior Palermo £££ The Excelsior dates back to 1891, when the building was created in Liberty style for the National Art Exposition. Since then, it has maintained its international flavour and appeal. There are 100 spacious rooms. ⓐ Via Marchese Ugo 3 ⓣ (091) 7909 ⓕ (091) 342 139 ⓦ www.excelsiorpalermo.it ⓝ Bus: 101

Posta £££ This ancient palace once belonged to a baroness. Its rooms are decorated with a splash of 1970s style. The prime location makes this a good choice for women travelling on their own. ⓐ Via Gagini 77 ⓣ (091) 587 338 ⓕ (091) 587 347 ⓦ www.hotelpostapalermo.it ⓝ Bus: 101, 107

Grand Hotel et Des Palmes £££–£££+ Located in the heart of the city, this is probably the top hotel in Palermo. The classic style and attentive staff make it a good choice for travellers for whom comfort is the priority. ⓐ Via Roma 398 ⓣ (091) 602 8111 ⓕ (091) 331 545 ⓦ www.hotel-despalmes.it ⓝ Bus: 101, 102, 103, 104

Ai Cavalieri Hotel £££+ This boutique hotel offers 35 rooms, some with balconies, free internet, breakfast, and is pet-friendly. Garage parking is available at an extra charge. ⓐ Via Sant'Oliva 8 ⓣ (091) 583 282 ⓕ (091) 612 6589 ⓦ www.aicavalierihotel.it ⓝ Linea Gialla (yellow line) bus

Grand Hotel Villa Igiea £££+ This 19th-century art nouveau masterpiece, 3 km (nearly 2 miles) north of the city in Aquasanta, was used as a summer resort by the Florio family, the first people

● *Grand Hotel Villa Igiea is as palacial as they come*

ACCOMMODATION

MAKING THE MOST OF PALERMO

to can tuna in Sicily. The interior was decorated by Italian art nouveau master Ernesto Basile. The hotel offers excellent service, elegant rooms with balconies, formal gardens and complimentary hourly shuttle service to and from the city centre. ⓐ Salita Belmonte 43 ⓣ (091) 631 2111 ⓕ (091) 547 654 ⓦ www.hotelvillaigieapalermo.com ⓝ Bus: 209, 210, 603

Hotel Principe di Villafranca £££+ An elegant boutique hotel in an upper-class residential neighbourhood. Rooms are decorated with works by local artists; breakfast and parking are included. ⓐ Via G Turrisi Colonna 4 ⓣ (091) 611 8523 ⓕ (091) 588 705 ⓦ www.principedivillafranca.it ⓝ Bus: 139, 702, 704

Massimo Plaza Hotel £££+ Located across from the Teatro Massimo, this elegant boutique hotel has been totally refurbished as part of the urban renewal of Palermo. Car park nearby. ⓐ Via Maqueda 437 ⓣ (091) 325 657 ⓕ (091) 325 711 ⓦ www.massimoplazahotel.com ⓝ Linea Rossa (red line) bus

Ucciardhome Hotel £££+ Located in the heart of the old city centre, close to Via della Libertà, this boutique hotel's soundproofed rooms are furnished in sleek, minimalist style. ⓐ Via Enrico Albanese 34–36 ⓣ (091) 348 426 ⓕ (091) 730 2738 ⓦ www.hotelucciardhome.com ⓝ Bus: 101, 102

HOSTELS
Baia del Corallo £ No frills, dormitory beds, shared bathrooms, but the main thing in its favour is its proximity to the beach. Located in Sferracavallo, 13 km (8 miles) and two buses from

ACCOMMODATION

Palermo. ⓐ Via Plauto 27 ⓣ (091) 679 7807 ⓕ (091) 691 2376 ⓔ palermo@ostellionline.org ⓝ Bus 101 from Stazione Centrale to the stadium, transfer to bus 628 and get off at the Hotel Bellevue stop after Sferracavallo

Casa Marconi ££ On the expensive side and a bit of a bus trek to get there, but it's modern, sparkling-clean and has only private rooms and bathrooms. ⓐ Via Monfenera 140 ⓣ (091) 657 0611 ⓕ (091) 657 0310 ⓦ www.casamarconi.it ⓝ Bus 246 from Stazione Centrale to the hospital at the end of the line, cross onto Via G Basile then turn left onto Via Monfenera

CAMPSITES

There are two campsites at Sferracavallo, a half-hour bus ride from Palermo; take bus 616 from Piazza Vittorio Veneto on the northern end of Via della Libertà. In view of the distance involved – 13 km (8 miles) – and the price of the hostels, unless you hanker for life under canvas it might be worth staying in a budget hotel in the city.

Degli Ulivi £ Very basic, cottages, bunk beds, coin-operated hot showers. ⓐ Via Pegaso 25 ⓣ/ⓕ (091) 533 021 ⓦ www.campingdegliulivi.com ⓔ mporion@libero.it ⓝ Bus: 628

Trinacria £ Across from the sea, small basic cottages that sleep between two and four people. Hot showers (included in rate) and a *pizzeria* on the premises. ⓐ Via Barcarello 25 ⓣ (091) 530 590 ⓦ www.campingtrinacria.it ⓝ Bus: 101 & 616

THE BEST OF PALERMO

Whether you are on a flying visit to Palermo or have a little more time to explore the city and its surroundings, there are some sights, places and experiences that you should not miss. For the best attractions for children, see pages 148–51.

TOP 10 ATTRACTIONS

- **Palazzo dei Normanni (Palace of the Normans)** Once the site of an Emir's palace and now home to the Sicilian Parliament (see page 73)

- **Cappella Palatina** Mosaic scenes of Christ in the magnificently decorated 12th-century chapel (see page 73)

- **Royal Apartments** A pad that's fit for a king – a king called Roger (see page 74)

- **Cattedrale** A huge Norman relic, with many later additions, that is impossible to miss in more ways that one (see page 65)

- **La Martorana & San Cataldo** Red golf-ball domes and another medieval church (see pages 66 and 68)

- **Galleria Regionale di Sicilia (Regional Gallery)** Fabulous works of art in one of the country's best galleries, which specialises in medieval art (see page 98)

- **Museo Archeologico Regionale** A temple to Palermo's history from the Phoenician to the Roman eras. Highlights are the carvings from the temples of Selinunte (see page 86)

- **Orto Botanico & Villa Giulia** Stop and smell the flowers at two oases near the city centre. The botanic garden displays some exotic specimens (see pages 80 and 83)

- **Museo Internazionale delle Marionette** Lots of puppets and even Punch and Judy in a museum that will fascinate both adults and children (see page 100)

- **La Zisa** See how the nobles lived and view the palace's collection of Islamic art (see page 88)

◐ *Aerial view of the city rooftops*

MAKING THE MOST OF PALERMO

Suggested itineraries

HALF-DAY: PALERMO IN A HURRY
To get a sense of Palermo's history, spend a few hours walking the narrow streets of the original town, the Quattro Canti, around the Palazzo dei Normanni (see page 73). Built by the Arabs in the 9th century as the Emir's palace, it was abandoned by them in 938, then rescued first by the Normans and later by the Spanish in the 17th century.

Continue exploring with a walk through the tiny streets of the Albergheria district. Bordered by the Via Maqueda and Via Vittorio Emanuele, this is a lively area day or night with cheap places to dine and drink.

If your visit to Palermo is in the evening, stroll the wide boulevards that surround illuminated monuments and cathedrals after dinner. Or take in a performance at the Teatro Massimo (see page 74), one of the many regional theatres, or head to the cinema.

1 DAY: TIME TO SEE A LITTLE MORE
Follow on the heels of the half-day itinerary above with tours of some of the city's beautiful churches.

The Cappella Palatina (see page 73) was the private chapel of Roger II. Its walls are entirely covered with magnificent 12th-century mosaics. The Cattedrale (see page 65) offers more Norman architecture and tombs of the Swabian and Norman royal families.

Also in that area are the churches of San Cataldo (see page 68), with its red golf-ball shaped domes and La Martorana (see page 66), considered by many to be the finest surviving building in the medieval city.

SUGGESTED ITINERARIES

2–3 DAYS: TIME TO SEE MUCH MORE
A longer stay means more time to explore areas outside the city centre. In La Kalsa (see page 96), the Arabic quarter near the sea, the aroma of spices emanating from the many cafés is sure to whet your appetite. The 15th-century Palazzo Abatellis and the Galleria Regionale di Sicilia (see page 98) combine to create a visual treat. Take a bus to the Museo Internazionale delle Marionette (see page 100). The superb castle, La Zisa (see page 88), offers a wonderful collection of Islamic art.

When it is time to take a break, settle yourself down in the delightful **Parco della Favorita** (Via Impertole Federico), admire the formal gardens and the Chinese-style pavilion, **Palazzina Cinese** ((091) 740 111), and people-watch.

LONGER: ENJOYING PALERMO TO THE FULL
You might consider short bus, train or ferry trips outside of Palermo. Sunbathe for a day in Mondello (see page 110), explore the Duomo in Monreale on the city's outskirts (see page 116), or head west an hour or so to the seaside towns of Trapani and Marsala (see page 124). Kick back and rest for a day or two on the tiny island of Ustica, 60 km (37 miles) northwest of Palermo. For a nature break hike through the Riserva Monte Pellegrino Naturale (Monte Pellegrino Nature Reserve, see page 150) and be rewarded with amazing views at the top.

◐ *Escape to Mondello if time permits*

MAKING THE MOST OF PALERMO

Something for nothing

You don't have to spend a lot on admission fees to see or learn about Palermo's culture. There are piazzas, parks and avenues lined with monuments, churches, fountains, murals, gorgeous architecture and colourful gardens that can be enjoyed for free.

● *Murals provide a colourful and free spectacle in the Albergheria quarter*

SOMETHING FOR NOTHING

In public parks watch or join in a football game, be entertained by street artists, sit on the steps of a centuries-old church overlooking a piazza, and participate in the best free show: people-watching. From June to September, city parks and open squares are venues for free theatre performances of musicals, ballet and folklore events.

All of Palermo's churches are free, offering a great opportunity to enjoy their liturgical art and magnificent interiors. An inexpensive bus ride will get you to the base of Monte Pellegrino where you can visit the chapel dedicated to Santa Rosalia, the patron saint of Palermo (see page 150), and enjoy expansive views of the city below.

Wine bars are all the rage here, putting out a free smorgasbord of food to tempt young professionals. So, get out the evening clothes and join them, as for the price of a drink you can dine well. During daylight walks or sightseeing treks through the city, be on the look out for cafés and bars that offer this, then return in the evening.

Festivals bring lots of free goods; concerts, parades, live theatre and fireworks displays to name a few. The summer is fraught with festivals, the largest one, Festino di Santa Rosalia (see page 10), lasts for six days in July. During this time the city almost shuts down to celebrate the life of Santa Rosalia, who saved Palermo from the plague in 1600. It is invaded by travelling theatrical and musical shows, all offering plays about the life of Santa Rosalia. The culmination comes with a monumental procession and fireworks display. February brings the baroque carnival (see page 8), celebrating Palermo's history with citywide masked balls and parades.

Food is a staple at any of the city's festivals; the streets and piazzas are clogged with kiosks of regional specialities, where you can sample for nothing or eat inexpensively.

MAKING THE MOST OF PALERMO

When it rains

A rainy day presents a good opportunity to explore some of Palermo's smaller, less crowded, out-of-the-way museums. Or to escape inclement weather and for a taste of something a little different – not to say slightly macabre – go underground into the catacombs or join a tour of the canals.

Located in the old section of the city behind the church of San Domenico, **Oratorio del Rosario di San Domenico** (✉ Via di Bambini 16 ✆ (091) 332 779) is adorned with some the best baroque sculpture in Palermo. Built in the 16th century by the Knights of Malta, its beauty derives from the fact that it was decorated by two absolute masters of their art: one was the genius of stucco sculpture, Giacomo Serpotta, who devoted his life to creating oratories like this; the other, the painter and designer Pietro Novelli, was very much a local lad made good. His finest achievement, the *Madonna of the Rosary* altarpiece is one of the city's all-time greatest pieces of art and is reason enough to visit the church, regardless of the weather. Housed in the beautiful Banco di Sicilia building, **Museo d'Arte e Archeologia** (✉ Via della Libertà 52 ✆ (091) 608 5974 ⓦ www.fondazionebancodisicilia.it) is a brilliant collection of paintings and artefacts. In fact, this is one of the very best museums in Sicily, and it will entrance you, whether you are a fan of what archaeology throws up or not. On display here are colourful pieces of Italian majolica dating back to the 16th century, an impressive collection of Greek vases, maps, rare coins, 19th-century paintings of seascapes by Antonino Leto and beautiful portraits of European women by Ettore de Maria Bergler. There are also some particularly wonderful Phoenician finds and some captivating Roman mosaics. Five minutes in here, you won't care

WHEN IT RAINS

if it's raining locusts outside! The **Catacombe dei Cappuccini** (Piazza Cappuccini 1 (091) 212 663), the crypts of the Capuchin convent (built in 1651), contain thousands of fully dressed mummified corpses of Capuchin friars, wealthy Palermitans, including women, and children that were buried there until 1881 when the custom was abolished. The site is both macabre and beautiful, with corpses on walls and in niches, many looking as if they are conversing with each other. A particularly beautiful and sad one is the corpse of a little girl, so perfectly embalmed that even her hair ribbon is still intact.

The tomb of Giuseppe Tomasi di Lampedusa, author of the famous Sicilian novel, *The Leopard*, is in the adjoining graveyard.

If a little bit of precipitation has put you in an aquatic mood, an answer to the question of what to do without getting wet is available in the form of the city's drainage system (stick with this wheeze: it's not as desperate as it sounds). Not to be missed, the Palermo Sottosopra are *guanat* (water conduits), that absorb moisture from the water table then run it for miles underground. First built in what was Persia in the 7th century, they were implemented in Europe after the fall of the Roman Empire. Palermo's conduits date from the Norman period. They were built by the *muganni*, or water masters, whose trade was handed down from father to son. Tours of the water conduits meet at various places in the city, and if you would like to join one then further information is available from the tourist office (see page 153) or from **Cooperativa Solidarieta** ((091) 580 433 www.cooperativasolidarieta.org). It is best to contact them a couple of days in advance, which, of course, assumes that you have access to a very reliable weather forecast; if the weather lets you down and stays sunny, it could be time to perform that rain dance.

MAKING THE MOST OF PALERMO

On arrival

TIME DIFFERENCE
Italy follows Central European Time (CET). During Daylight Saving Time (end Mar–end Oct), the clocks are put ahead one hour.

ARRIVING
By air
Palermo's airport, **Falcone e Borsellino** (☏ (091) 702 0111 🌐 www.gesap.it), is 35 km (22 miles) north of Palermo and is served by many international and domestic airlines. Inside the terminal there are cash machines, money exchange bureaux (🕒 09.00–16.00 Mon–Fri, closed Sat & Sun),

> **IF YOU GET LOST, TRY …**
>
> **Excuse me, do you speak English?**
> Mi scusi, parla inglese?
> *Mee skoozee, pahrlah eenglehzeh?*
>
> **Excuse me, is this the right way to the old town/the city centre/the tourist office/the station/the bus station?**
> Mi scusi, è questa la strada per la città vecchia/al centro città/ l'ufficio informazioni turistiche/alla stazione ferroviaria/ alla stazione degli autobus?
> *Mee skoozee, eh kwehstah lah strahda pehr lah cheetta vehkyah/ ahl chentraw cheetteh/looffeechaw eenforrmahtsyawnee tooreesteekeh/ahlla statsyoneh fehrohveeahreeyah/ ahlla statsyoneh delee ahootawboos?*

ON ARRIVAL

car hire, and an English-speaking tourist office (❶ (091) 591 698 ❷ 08.00–20.00 Mon–Sat, 08.00–14.00 Sun), where you can pick up free city and public transport maps which can also be purchased at newspaper stands around the city.

Airport taxis (❶ (091) 225 455 ❷ 06.00–00.00) wait at the kerbside by the arrivals terminal. It is a 40-minute trip into the city, costing around €50. For airport buses, phone ❶ (091) 580 457. The Prestia e Comandè link bus located outside the arrivals terminal stops at Via Lazio, Piazza Ruggero Settimo in front of the Politeama Hotel, ending at Stazione Centrale. The buses run every 30 minutes from 06.30–00.00 (airport to city centre) and 05.00–23.00 (city centre to airport). The trip takes 50 minutes and costs €5.30.

Prestia e Comande ❸ Largo Siviglia 5 ❶ (091) 586 351 or 580 457 ❿ www.prestia-comande.it

The airport is also connected to the city's main train station, Palermo Stazione Centrale by the **Trinacria Express** (❶ (091) 892 021), a direct train line. Trains take approximately 55 minutes, and run from 06.20–20.50 (airport to city centre) and 06.30–19.30 (city centre to airport). Tickets cost €5.

By rail

Palermo's main train station is **Stazione Centrale** (❶ 603 111 ❿ www.trenitalia.it). The train from mainland Italy and Italian State Railways (Ferrovie dello Santo) services cross the Straits of Messina. The train drives straight onto the ferry – the cost of which is included in the train ticket. If you are travelling from within Sicily there is limited train service to Palermo from Messina (three hours), Caltinissetta (two hours) and Catania (three hours). All arrive at Stazione Centrale. For information and tickets contact:

MAKING THE MOST OF PALERMO

Italian State Railways – Ferrovie dello Stato @ Piazza della Croce Rossa 1, Rome W www.treniitalia.com
Eurostar T 0870 518 6186 W www.eurostar.com
Rail Europe T 0870 584 8848 W www.raileurope.co.uk
Travel Cuts T (020) 7255 1944

By road

A daily bus service from Rome departs **Stazione Tiburtina** (T (064) 423 4780) at 09.00, arriving at Palermo's Via Balsamo bus station (there are, in fact, three stations on this road) 12 hours later. Cost is approximately €35.50 one way, or €60.50 for the round trip. This service is available from:

Segesta Internazionale Bus T (091) 300 556 (weekdays); (091) 320 757 (Sat & Sun and public holidays).

Several other bus companies offer services from other major cities in Sicily to and from Palermo:

Cuffaro @ Via Balsamo 13 T (091) 616 1510
SAIS @ Via Balsamo 16 T (091) 616 6028
Segesta @ Via Balsamo 26 T (091) 616 7919

Avoid driving in Palermo as the traffic is horrendous and the streets are narrow and crowded. And if that isn't enough, another problem is parking. In the city proper there are only four municipal car parks. Be warned, a city car park might have special arrangements with nearby hotels, giving hotel guests priority parking. Large car parks are found on the outskirts of Palermo, which could mean a long walk or bus ride into the city centre. The cost for most car parks is approximately €30 for 24 hours.

If you must drive, the major thoroughfares are the A19, A20 and the A29. As you approach Palermo these join a loop road, the Viale

ON ARRIVAL

Regionale Siciliana, and from this several marked exits can be taken into the city.

By water
One of the prettiest and most leisurely ways of arriving in Palermo is by sea. Ferries leave from various mainland cities.
Genova–Palermo, operated by Grandi Navi Veloci; one ferry daily, a 20-hour journey.
Livorno–Palermo, operated by Grandi Navi Veloci; three times a week, a 17-hour journey.
Naples–Palermo, operated by Tirrenia Line; one car ferry daily, an 11-hour journey.
Naples–Palermo, operated by SNAV; one catamaran daily mid-April to early October, a 4-hour journey.

Agents for the above Italian ferry services are:
Grandi Navi Veloci In the UK: c/o Viamare (020) 7431 4560
www.viamare.com; in Italy: Via Fieschi 17, Genova (010) 55 (091)
www.gnv.it
SNAV In the UK: c/o Viamare (020) 7431 4560 www.viamare.com;
in Italy: Stazione Marittima, Napoli (081) 428 5111; from outside
Italy: www.snav.it mergelli@tin.it
Tirrenia Line In the UK: c/o SMS Travel (020) 7373 6548
www.tirrenia.it; in Italy Molo Angioino, Napoli (199) 123 199
from Italy, or (081) 317 2999 from outside Italy www.gruppotirrenia.it

FINDING YOUR FEET
If you live in one of Western Europe's larger towns or cities, you might well find that, initially, you have to make a determined – but pleasurable – effort to slow down a bit in order to adjust to

MAKING THE MOST OF PALERMO

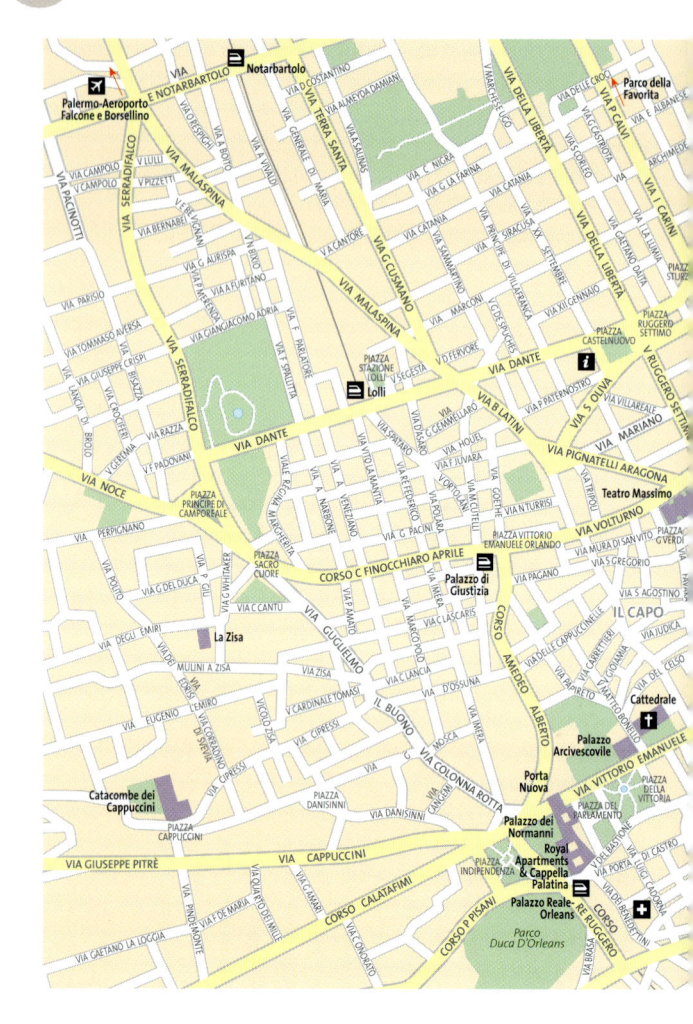

ON ARRIVAL

MAKING THE MOST OF PALERMO

Palermo's comparatively laid-back tempo. A little decompression time will enable you to settle into the local groove. It would be a good idea, on your first full day in Palermo, to try to factor in some early morning down time. Find a centrally located park or café where you can relax and acquaint yourself with the city. By doing this, you will have a chance to notice how beautiful, spacious and elegant Palermo is. You will also be able to observe the locals (and how beautiful, gracious and elegant quite a high proportion of them are!), and begin to get a feel for the pace at which they live.

To make the most of your visit, before you travel you should study your city and transport maps. Treat Palermo as you would any other metropolitan city, and don't let its beauty seduce you into being careless of your personal safety. In Palermo, you don't need to be obsessive about this, and a few common-sense rules should keep you out of trouble. Be conscious of your surroundings at all times; do not carry or show large sums of money, cameras or jewellery. After dark keep away from areas around the train or bus stations, and late at night take taxis or walk only in well lit, heavily populated areas. Palermo has its share of motor scooters, and be warned – a few of their drivers are experts at snatching dangling purses, cameras or necklaces from pedestrians. In other words, try not to look like a tourist, and keep all valuables close to you and out of sight. Ostentatious wealth is best avoided, as is ostentatious tipsiness.

ORIENTATION

The medieval street system is alive and well in Palermo, making it quite easy for visitors to get lost – but this eventuality is far from being inevitable – in fact, it can easily be avoided. Note your starting location by remembering a major landmark or through street, and always carry a city map. The maps in this book show the main sights and streets, but some of the places listed are on smaller streets, so if you are planning a longer stay in the city it is worth acquiring a detailed map from a local bookshop or news-stand.

Begin your sightseeing in the Quattro Canti, the crossroads of Palermo's major streets; Via Maqueda, Via Vittorio Emanuele and Via Roma. The Quattro (formerly Piazza Vigliena) is the focal point of the city centre's oldest district and is a perfect orientation spot. This is the city's most heavily concentrated area of historic churches, palaces and museums, many of which are within walking distance from each other. Of course, most of these establishments have 'you are here' maps that will help you, not to mention attentive staff whose weekly wage depends on their re-orientating the temporarily bewildered. (Indeed, if you do get a little lost, don't panic and don't hesitate to ask a local person for help.) Most Palermitans will be only too eager to help you, and to demonstrate their English.

Surrounding the Quattro Canti are the Ballaro and Vucciria market areas, good places to pick up a meal to go. If you get lost you can ask for directions in any of the area's numerous shops or restaurants, or use the Via Maqueda as your guide – it crosses Palermo, becoming the Via della Libertà in the modern section of the city.

GETTING AROUND

Although walking is strongly advised as being by far the most enjoyable way of getting around in Palermo, you may tire at some point and want to use public transport. (Incidentally, city listings in this guide that do not have public transport connections listed in their practical information can be assumed to be most easily reached on foot.) Happily, the city has extensive and easy-to-use public transport facilities, especially when it comes to travelling by bus. **AMAT** city buses (☎ (199) 240 800 ⓦ www.amat.pa.it) cover Palermo as well as Monreale, Mondello and beyond. You can purchase a flat-fare ticket, €1 valid on any bus for two hours, or an all-day ticket for €3.50. AMAT kiosks are at Stazione Centrale (see page 49), Piazza Ruggero Settimo and Piazza Verdi, or anywhere you see the sign 'Vendita Biglietti AMAT'. All you need to do is validate one in the machine on the bus as you start your journey. For all-day tickets do it only on the first ride.

If you want to do a whistle-stop tour of the must-sees, two minibus services loop the city and take in all its most popular tourist sights; **Linea Gialla** (Yellow Line; 07.30–19.30) and **Linea Rossa** (Red Line; 07.30–20.20). Tickets are available at AMAT ticket kiosks, €1 for two hours, or €3.50 for the day. City buses run from 04.00–23.00. Bus ranks are outside the train station and at various points along Via Vittorio Emanuele and Via della Libertà.

Two reliable taxi firms are:

Audioradio Taxi (☎ (091) 513 311 or (091) 513 198)
Radio Taxi Trinacria (☎ (091) 682 5441 or (091) 225 455)

Taxi ranks are found at:

Civic Hospital ☎ (091) 486 981
Lido di Mondello ☎ (091) 513 311
Massimo, Piazza G Verdi ☎ (091) 320 184
Piazza Indipendenza ☎ (091) 422 703
Politeama ☎ (091) 588 133
Stazione Central FS ☎ (091) 616 2001
Stazione Notarbartolo FS ☎ (091) 343 506
Via Eman Notabartolo ☎ (091) 625 1672
Via Malta ☎ (091) 616 2000 or (091) 231 000

ON ARRIVAL

▲ *If you do get caught in the rain, there are plenty of buses*

MAKING THE MOST OF PALERMO

CAR HIRE

A piece of paramount advice – do not drive in Palermo city itself. That said, the best way to explore the countryside is by car. When making your airline reservation, enquire if an air/car package is offered.

There are six car-hire agencies at the airport that also have offices in the city.

Avis ❶ (091) 591 684 ⓦ www.avis.co.uk/CarHire/Europe/Italy/Palermo
Europcar ❶ (091) 591 688 ⓦ www.europcar.it
Hertz ❶ (091) 213 112 ⓦ www.hertz.it
Holiday Car Rental ❶ (091) 591 687 ⓦ www.holidaycarrental.biz
Maggiore Car Rental ❶ (091) 591 681 ⓦ www.maggiore.it
Sicily by Car ❶ (091) 591 250 ⓦ www.sbc.it

To check rates or reserve, go to ⓦ www.carhire.co.uk/car-hire/palermo-airport.html or ⓦ www.hispacar.com

Once you have your documents, take time to familiarise yourself with the vehicle. Anyone who is accustomed to driving on the left will have a problem adjusting to roundabouts, traffic and two-lane highways, so stay alert and go slow.

◐ *Palermo has stunning religious statuary*

THE CITY OF
Palermo

THE CITY

Quattro Canti & the Albergheria

A spacious octagon marks the intersection of the city's two main streets, Via Vittorio Emanuele and Via Maqueda. Built in 1611, Piazza Vigliena, or, as it is better known, the Quattro Canti, is not really a piazza but more a set of baroque crossroads that divide the city into quadrants. A short walk in any direction brings you to some of Palermo's most elegant piazzas, buildings and four magnificent churches: San Giuseppe dei Teatini (see page 70), Santa Caterina (see page 70), San Cataldo (see page 68) and La Martorana (see page 66).

Also in the Quattro is the University, making the area a haven for students and good, cheap cafés and bars.

The Albergheria district, bounded by the Via Maqueda and Via Vittorio Emanuele, has its own ambience, having been little changed for several hundred years.

SIGHTS & ATTRACTIONS

The Albergheria
Within this district, Via Maqueda is lined with beautiful *palazzos*, such as the 18th-century Palazzo Santa Croce, behind which is a neighbourhood of narrow streets, cafés, markets and churches. Most of this was bombed in 1943 and has never been repaired, which only serves to add to the uniqueness of the area.

Il Capo
The apses of the Cattedrale border the Capo quarter, one of the oldest areas of Palermo. The only bit of green space in this congested, run-down area is the tiny, graceful Piazza Monte di Pietà, which is planted with trees and ringed by neighbourhood bars. There really

Quattro Canti & the Albergheria

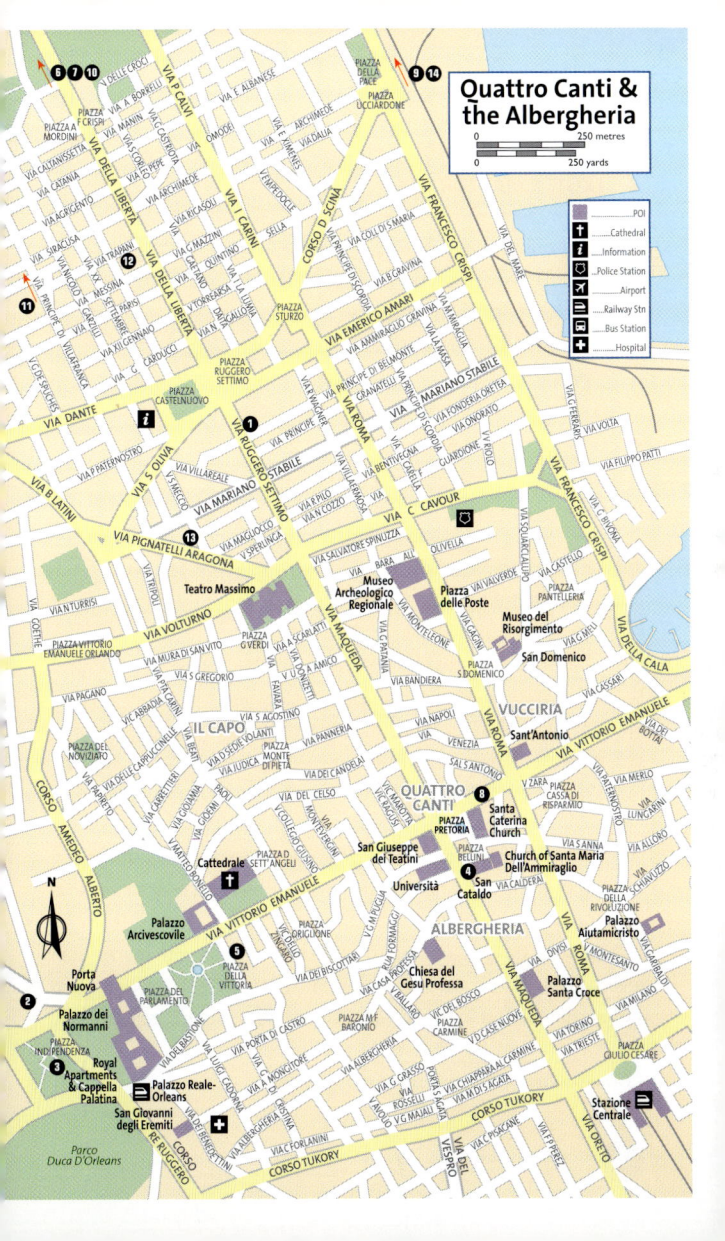

0 — 250 metres
0 — 250 yards

- POI
- Cathedral
- Information
- Police Station
- Airport
- Railway Stn
- Bus Station
- Hospital

THE CITY

> **FRUTTA MARTORANA**
>
> *Frutta Martorana*, also known as *paste reale* and one of the most typical kinds of Sicilian *pasticcerie*, is named after the church that bears the same name. According to tradition, the origins of this delicacy can be traced back to medieval times when every convent specialised in making a different kind of confectionery. The ones made by the Benedictine convent of La Martorana (see page 66) in early November for the feast day of All Saints were of marzipan, shaped and coloured to resemble different kinds of fruits. The tradition continues today; during the Festival of the Dead at the beginning of November (see page 11), the district between Via Salvatore Spinuzza and Piazza Olivella is invaded by brightly coloured stalls selling *frutta martorana* dolls and children's toys made from sugar.
>
> Marzipan is also of medieval origin; the term is derived from the Arabic *mauthaban*, which originally denoted a coin, then a unit of measurement and finally the container used to store the paste which is made with almonds, sugar and egg whites.

is not much to see here save for a few decaying palaces, but, after looking at grand buildings, strolling here gives you a peek at a typical Palermo neighbourhood.

One alley, Via Porta Carini, is packed on either side with market stalls giving it the look of an Arab souk. Climb past decrepit buildings and closed churches, up to the Porta Carini, one of the city's medieval gates.

◑ *Quattro Canti is the impressive heart of the city*

QUATTRO CANTI & THE ALBERGHERIA

THE CITY

The market extends west to the edge of the Capo district and east along Via Sant'Agostino, where you will find the **Church of Sant'Agostino** (ℹ (091) 584 632), built in the 13th century by the Chiaramonte and Sclafani families, scions of Sicilian aristocracy. The interior is decorated with some fine stuccoes by Giacomo Serpotta. On the Via Sant'Agostino side of the building, behind the market stalls, is a deteriorating 15th-century doorway attributed

▼ *Palermo's Cattedrale was begun in the 12th century, but has later additions*

QUATTRO CANTI & THE ALBERGHERIA

to Domenico Gagini, one of a dynasty of skilled medieval sculptors who decorated many buildings in Sicily with their artwork.

Cattedrale
Palermo's glorious cathedral was founded in the 12th century by the English archbishop Gualtiero Offamiglio (Walter of the Mill), and was to be his base of operations – he didn't get the chance to use it as he died several centuries before it was finished.

THE CITY

The Catalan Gothic south porch was added in the 15th century. Among its Gothic decorations are symbols of the four evangelists, Saints Matthew, Mark, Luke and John, on the outer wall. Other works of striking ornamentation are the beautiful hand-carved wooden doors and the apses which retain original Norman details.

The dome was added in the 18th century when the church was totally refurbished. Of interest in the bland interior are the tombs containing the remains of some of Sicily's Swabian and Norman monarchs: Frederick II and his wife Constance, Henry VI and, at the rear, Roger II and his daughter Costanza d'Altavilla. In the small chapel to the right of the choir altar are the remains of St Rosalia, the patron saint of Palermo.

The treasury, or *tesoro*, has an impressive collection of rings, necklaces and the Imperial Gold Crown, which is set with precious stones, pearls and enamels. There's also a carved ivory staff made in Sicily in the 17th century and jewels belonging to Queen Costanza of Aragon. Of particular note is a classical Roman sarcophagus decorated with the figures of the nine Muses and Apollo. ⓐ Via Vittorio Emanuele ⓣ (091) 334 376 ⓦ www.cattedrale.palermo.it ⓑ 07.00–19.00 Mon–Sat, 08.00–13.30 Sun. Admission charge

Church of Santa Maria Dell'Ammiraglio (La Martorana Church)

The church's official name is Saint Mary's of the Admiral. It was built in 1143 by King Roger II's admiral, George of Antioch. Throughout the centuries the church has undergone many alterations. Peter of Aragon was crowned king here, and under the Spanish the church was given to a convent that was founded by Eloisa Martorana. It is from her that it derives its name: La Martorana.

Unfortunately, in the 17th century most of La Martorana's original Arab-Norman construction was scaled off and replaced with baroque.

QUATTRO CANTI & THE ALBERGHERIA

What does exist from that period are the church's spectacular mosaics: *King Roger Being Crowned by Christ*, *The Nativity* and *The Passing Away of the Virgin*. These are just three of the many that decorate the interior spaces and the mosaics are attributed to master Byzantine craftsmen brought to Sicily from Constantinople by King Roger II.

The remaining exterior Norman elements are the bell tower, the domed roof and the external walls, with blind arcading around the windows. ⓐ Piazza Bellini 2, adjacent to Piazza Pretoria ⓘ (091) 616 1692 ⓛ 09.30–13.00, 15.30–18.30 Mon–Sat, 08.30–13.00 Sun ⓑ Bus: 101, 102

Palazzo Arcivescovile

At the western end of the Cattedrale is the Palazzo Archivescovile, at one time the archbishop's palace. The *palazzo* is entered through a 15th-century gateway (the Porta Nuova) and inside is the **Museo Diocesano** (ⓘ (091) 607 7111), which brings together various artworks from the cathedral and churches destroyed in World War II. The museum is staffed by volunteers, making the hours erratic – if it's closed you should still be able to take a look around in the courtyard. As you exit the *palazzo* turn left up Via Bonello, where there is a lively antiques market, Mercato delle Pulci in Piazza Peranni. ⓐ Via Matteo Bonello 2 ⓘ (091) 607 7215 ⓛ 09.30–13.30 Tues–Fri, Sun, 10.00–18.00 Sat, closed Mon ⓑ Bus: 104. Admission charge

Piazza Pretoria

Cross Via Maqueda to reach this lovely piazza centred with a magnificent fountain. Its 16 statues are divided by four sets of stairs leading to the largest fountain in the centre. The fountain was sculpted in 1555 by Francesco Camilliani and originally stood in the Tuscan villa of the Viceroy Don Pedro de Toledo. The Viceroy's son sold the fountain to the city of Palermo in 1574. It was shipped here piece by piece and installed in front of the Municipio (Town Hall).

San Cataldo
Although not on as grand a scale as La Martorana (see page 66), this dignified little 12th-century chapel, with its red golf-ball shaped domes, holds its own with its simplistic beauty. The church was never decorated, save for the crenellations around the roof. In the 18th century it was Palermo's post office. Surrounding it is a pretty mosaic walkway, a pinch of colour in the otherwise bare Piazza Bellini. ⓐ Piazza Bellini 2, adjacent to La Martorana ⓣ (091) 616 1692 ⓛ 09.30–17.00 Tues–Fri, 09.00–13.00 Sat & Sun, closed Mon ⓝ Bus: 101, 102. Admission charge

San Giovanni degli Eremiti (Church of Saint John of the Hermits)
Situated in a lovely and peaceful garden near the Palazzo dei Normanni (see page 73), is the deconsecrated church of San Giovanni degli Eremiti. Built in 1132 on the site of an earlier mosque, its red roof with five squat domes is clearly the work of Moorish craftsmen. The church was a favourite of its founder, King Roger II, who granted the monks of San Giovanni 21 barrels of tuna a year, a special gift considering that food products were controlled by the Crown at that time. The lacklustre interior has only a few broken frescoes. All that is left of the adjacent monastery are the 13th-century cloisters, whose twin columns surround a small garden. ⓐ Via dei Benedettini ⓣ (091) 651 5019 ⓛ 09.00–13.00, 15.00–19.00 Mon–Sat, 09.00–13.00 Sun ⓝ Bus: 109, 318. Admission charge

---

◐ *The exterior of San Cataldo is bare save for those distinctive red domes*

QUATTRO CANTI & THE ALBERGHERIA

THE CITY

San Giuseppe dei Teatini
Don't let the simple façade of this magnificent 17th-century church fool you. The church was designed by Giacomo Besio in 1612, and its interior, laid out in a Latin cross form, is a treasure trove of details; everything from a stunning encrusted ceiling, white and gold decorations and frescos, to 22 enormous stucco columns supporting the great dome, mostly restored from bomb damage in 1943. ⓐ Via Vittorio Emanuele ⓣ (091) 331 239 ⓦ www.sangiuseppeteatini.arcidiocesi.palermo.it ⓛ 07.30–12.00, 17.30–20.00 Mon–Sat, 08.30–13.00, 18.00–20.00 Sun ⓝ Bus: 101, 102, 103

Santa Caterina Church
Flanking the piazza is the church of Santa Caterina, a fine example of Sicilian baroque architecture, the inside of which is bright with colour; deep reds and brilliant yellows filling crevices behind sculpted cherubs, Madonnas, lions and eagles. There's a marble panel (on the right as you enter one of the smaller chapels) depicting Jonah about to be swallowed by a ferocious whale.
ⓐ Piazza Bellini ⓝ Bus: 101, 102, 103

Via Vittorio Emanuele and the Porta Nuova
If you return to the main street, you will note on the northern side of the Royal Palace the commanding Porta Nuova. Built in 1535, it celebrates Charles V's Tunisian exploits with carvings of Arabic figures.

▶ *Quattro Canti, literally four corners, equals spectacular architecture*

QUATTRO CANTI & THE ALBERGHERIA

THE CITY

QUATTRO CANTI & THE ALBERGHERIA

CULTURE

Cappella Palatina

The chapel is considered by many to be the crown jewel of central Palermo. Built between 1132 and 1143 as the private chapel of Roger II, its magnificent interior, the cupola, three apses and nave are completely covered in outstanding mosaics. The oldest, completed in 1150 by Byzantine artists, are in the cupola and apses. Those in the nave, depicting the Old and New Testaments, were completed 20 years later by local craftsmen. The colours are so vivid they seem to leap out at you. Scenes depict Christ blessing, open book in hand, and Christ enthroned between Peter (to whom the chapel is dedicated) and Paul.

The Arab history of Palermo comes out in the chapel's Arabic ceiling with its carved wooden stalactites, patterned marble floor and, by the pulpit, an extraordinary, intricately carved Norman candlestick measuring 4 m (13 ft) in height. ⓐ Piazza del Parlamento ⓘ (091) 626 2833 ⓒ 08.30–12.00, 14.00–17.00 Mon–Sat, 08.30–12.30 Sun ⓑ Bus: 104, 105, 108, 109, 110, 118, 304, 309

Palazzo dei Normanni (Palace of the Normans)

A royal palace has occupied this high ground since the 9th century when the Arabs built a fortress for the Emir. In 938 they abandoned it, transferring the Emir's residence, for security reasons, to the Kalsa. Then came the Normans, who enlarged it, turning the fortress into a *palazzo* and filling the interior with magnificent medieval European courts. In the 17th century the Spanish added the *palazzo*'s long porch. Today, little remains of the original Arab-Norman structure.

◀ *Mosaics – some dating back to the 12th century – decorate Capella Palatina*

THE CITY

There is limited public access to the building as it now houses the Sicilian Parliament. ⓐ Piazza Indipendenza ⓣ (091) 705 7003 ⓛ 09.00–12.00 Mon, Fri & Sat, 08.30–12.00 Sun (other days by prior arrangement) ⓑ Bus: 104, 105, 108, 109, 110, 118, 304, 309

The Royal Apartments

It is now only possible to make a guided visit to the Sala di Ruggero (Roger's Room). One of the original parts of the *palazzo*, it is covered with fantastic 12th-century mosaics depicting hunting scenes. As the apartments constitute a brief visit, it is best to do this first before descending one floor to the wonderful Cappella. ⓐ Piazza del Parlamento ⓣ (091) 705 7003 ⓛ 09.00–12.00 Mon, Fri & Sat (other days by prior arrangement) ⓑ Bus: 104, 105, 108, 109, 110, 118, 304, 309

Teatro Massimo

Built in 1875 by Giovanni Battista Basile, whose neoclassical design is said to have been influenced by Charles Garnier's contemporary plans for the Paris Opera, it was finished by Basile's son Ernesto, who added the two distinctive Liberty-style kiosks in front of the theatre. The one on the right, built of wood and wrought iron, is the Vicari al Massimo Kiosk, while the one on the left, made of iron, is the Ribaudo Kiosk.

The interior is richly gilded with pink marble, and colours of rich reds, blues and golds grace the walls of the theatre and the Sala Pompeiana, where the nobility once gathered before a performance. In the auditorium is a massive domed ceiling carved into the shape of a flower.

For many years the opera house was the centre of high society in Palermo, with a grand selection of musical performers to its credit. You don't have to attend a performance to appreciate its

QUATTRO CANTI & THE ALBERGHERIA

beauty; guided tours in English are conducted throughout the year, except during rehearsals. ⓐ Piazza Verde ⓣ (091) 605 3515 ⓦ www.teatromassimo.it ⓛ Guided tours in English 10.00–16.00 every 30 mins Tues–Sun, closed Mon ⓝ Bus: 101, 102, 103, 104, 107, 122, 125. Admission charge

RETAIL THERAPY

Palermo has its share of shops, everything from haute couture to 'gently used' fashions from designer labels. There are many shops specialising in ceramics, art, wine, needlepoint, embroidered fabrics and linens. Some visitors come to Palermo just to purchase ceramics.

DeSimone This family-owned business creates beautiful tiles with scenes of the Sicilian countryside, seascapes and landscapes. ⓐ Via Lanza di Scalea 960 ⓣ (091) 671 1005 ⓛ 08.30–13.00, 14.00–17.30 Mon–Fri, closed Sat & Sun ⓝ Bus: 662, 619

Frette Frette's high thread-count sheets and ultra soft linens are reportedly used at the Vatican. Not only does that mean that they are famous, it also means high prices – but they're worth it. ⓐ Via Ruggero Settimo 12 ⓣ (091) 585 166 ⓛ 09.00–13.00, 15.30–20.00 Mon–Fri, 09.00–13.00, 16.00–20.00 Sat, closed Sun ⓝ Bus: 101, 102, 103, 124

Libreria Altro Quandro Along with the usual bestsellers, you will find a good amount of revolutionary, socialist and general books here. Being Sicily, gay books are upstairs, tucked away in the back of the shop. ⓐ Via Vittorio Emanuele 125 ⓣ (091) 611 4732 ⓛ 07.00–13.30, 16.00–19.30 Mon–Fri, 09.00–13.00, 16.00–20.00 Sat, closed Sun ⓝ Bus: 103, 104, 105, 108, 110, 139, 224, 225, 389, 824

THE CITY

Pasticceria Alba Palermo's leading pastry shop, where you can buy wonderful cakes and gifts to bring home, as well as things to eat on the spot. ⓐ Piazza Don Bosco 7c ⓣ (091) 309 016 ⓦ www.baralba.it ⓛ 07.00–23.00 Tues–Sun (winter); 07.00–00.00 Tues–Sun (summer), closed Mon ⓝ Bus: 104, 107

TAKING A BREAK

After feeding your senses on culture and shopping comes the time to re-fuel the body in the middle of the day. The old section of Palermo offers a host of cafés, *pizzerias* (more pizza is eaten in Palermo than in any other part of Italy), and ice cream palaces.

Antico Caffè Spinnato £ ❶ Quite simply, one of the best bars in Italy, and it does delicious snacks. Have your coffee standing up at the bar if you want to avoid the cover charge. ⓐ Via Principe di Belmonte 115 ⓣ (091) 583 231 ⓛ 07.00–01.00 ⓝ Bus: 107

Pasticceria Cappello £ ❷ A trip to this award-winning *pasticceria* is a must if you're a fan of Sicilian pastries. ⓐ Via Colonna Rotta 68 ⓣ (091) 489 601 ⓦ www.pasticceriacappello.it ⓛ 07.00–22.00 Thur–Tues, closed Wed ⓝ Bus: 101; Linea Gialla (yellow line) bus

Pasticceria Santoro £ ❸ Near the Palazzo dei Normanni on the edge of a wooded piazza. A shady respite on a hot day of sightseeing. ⓐ Piazza Indipendenza ⓣ (091) 422 086 ⓛ 06.30–22.00 ⓝ Bus: 104, 105, 108, 109, 110, 118, 304, 309

Bellini £–££ ❹ Housed at the back of the Teatro Bellini, the large pizza ovens are operating all day. At night sit at outdoor tables

QUATTRO CANTI & THE ALBERGHERIA

Just one of the many mouthwatering cakes from Pasticceria Cappello

underneath La Martorana church – one of the city's most romantic locations. Piazza Bellini (091) 616 5691 10.00–22.00 Thur–Tues, closed Wed Bus: 101, 102

Trattoria Normanni £–££ The speciality dish is *spaghetti al Normanni*, a wonderful mix of shrimps, aubergines, fresh vegetables and grated peanuts. Piazza della Vittoria 25 (at the southern end of Via San Francesco) (091) 651 6011 12.00–15.00, 19.30–23.00 Mon–Sat, closed Sun Bus: 104, 105, 108, 110, 118, 304, 309

AFTER DARK

The Quattro Canti and Albergheria areas are lovely to stroll in at night. Most of the *palazzos* and churches are illuminated, adding to the romance of the streets and avenues.

THE CITY

L'Antica Borgata £ ❻ A *pizzeria* offering a choice of more than 140 pizzas, including their speciality, *pizza all'insalata* – pizza topped with salad. ⓐ Via Africa 6–7 ⓣ (091) 670 1028 ⓛ 18.00–00.00 Tues–Sun, closed Mon ⓝ Bus: 118, 164

161 Bar & Restaurant ££ ❼ One for the younger crowd, 161 combines a restaurant with an 'American-style' lounge bar, featuring regular special events, DJs and parties. ⓐ Via della Libertà 161 ⓣ (091) 345 949 ⓦ www.welove161.it ⓛ 19.30–01.00 Tues–Sun, closed Mon ⓝ Bus: 101, 806, 103

Al Santa Caterina ££ ❽ Housed in a 16th-century *palazzo*, this intimate restaurant offers good Sicilian fare. Dine under the stars on a balcony overlooking the street. ⓐ Via Vittorio Emanuele 254 ⓣ (091) 662 2094 ⓛ 19.30–23.00 Thur–Tues, closed Wed ⓝ Bus: 101, 102

Era Ora Vintage ££ ❾ *Pizzeria* and restaurant, close to the seafront. Try the mixed fried fish. ⓐ Via Torre 26 ⓣ (091) 684 1843 ⓦ www.ristoranteeraora.com ⓛ 12.30–15.00, 19.00–23.00 ⓝ Bus: 544

Il Gattopardo ££ ❿ If the Palermo's traditional seafood dishes are getting too much for you, try the 'Scozzese' pizza on offer at this *pizzeria*/restaurant – it's topped with Scottish salmon. ⓐ Via Gabriele D'Annunzio 42 ⓣ (091) 730 0563 ⓦ www.ristoranteilgattopardo.it ⓛ 12.00–15.00, 19.30–23.00 ⓝ Linea Campania (bus)

Hirsch ££ ⓫ For a change from the Sicilian diet, try this German restaurant that offers a range of *schnitzel*, sausages and ostrich steaks. ⓐ Via Almeyda Damiani 32a ⓣ (091) 347 825 ⓛ 12.30–15.00, 19.00–23.00 ⓝ Bus: 103, 106

QUATTRO CANTI & THE ALBERGHERIA

Ristorante Régine ££ ⓬ Try the *scafazzé* – a dessert made with ricotta – at this charming restaurant run by three brothers. ⓐ Via Trapani 4a ⓣ (091) 586 566 ⓦ www.ristoranteregine.it ⓛ 19.00–23.00 Tues–Sun, closed Mon ⓝ Linea Rossa (red line) bus

Ristorante Tosca ££ ⓭ A restaurant that also offers a tempting range of pizzas, with a special Sicilian menu on Thursday evenings. ⓐ Via Pignatelli Aragona 70 ⓣ (091) 584 751 ⓦ www.ristorante-tosca.it ⓛ 19.00–23.00 Tues–Sat, 12.00–15.00, 19.00–23.00 Sun, closed Mon ⓝ Bus: 108

Bye Bye Blues £££ ⓮ Run by a husband and wife team: she is the chef, and he is the sommelier. Their menu changes every few months, so see their website for the latest delicious creations. ⓐ Via del Garofalo 23 ⓣ (091) 684 1415 ⓦ www.byebyeblues.it ⓛ 19.00–23.00 Wed–Mon, closed Tues ⓝ Bus: 544

● *Comfy lounge bar at 161 Bar & Restaurant*

THE CITY

Via Roma & the Vucciria

Starting at the Stazione Centrale and ending at Piazza Sturzo, Via Roma is a 20th-century addition to Palermo. Connected to Via Maqueda by several narrow alleys this area is not particularly beautiful or interesting, consisting of tall granite apartment blocks with hotels. The one break in this granite and cement jungle is Via Divisi to the east, a narrow street full of bicycle shops.

The surrounding area's retail commodities are grouped according to their trade; ironmongery, children's clothes and ceramics all have their own individual spots. After this, Via Roma is all clothes and shoe shops, with a few cafés and restaurants.

SIGHTS & ATTRACTIONS

Orto Botanico

This beautiful space is a favourite with Palermitans. The gardens and water lily pond were laid out in 1795. The most impressive specimen is the 150-year-old banyan tree with its gigantic roots sprawling over the ground. Growing here are species of plants from all over the world. In the spring they are covered with brilliant pink flowers which turn into fruit. ⓐ Via Abramo Lincoln 2b ⓘ (091) 623 8241 ⓛ 09.00–20.00 Mon–Fri, 09.00–13.00 Sat & Sun ⓝ Bus: 139, 211, 221, 224, 226, 227. Admission charge

Piazza Marina

It was the Arabs who did the world a favour and introduced gardens to Palermo. The Normans expanded on this with their parklands and summer palaces. In the heart of Palermo, at Piazza Marina, lies the Giardino (Garden) Garibaldi, the walks of which are lined with banyan

Via Roma & the Vucciria
250 metres
250 yards
Porto
N
Stazione Marittima
BANCHINA SAMMUZZO
La Cala
POI
Cathedral
Information
Police Station
Airport
Railway Stn
Bus Station
Hospital
PIAZZA DELLA PACE
PIAZZA UCCIARDONE
VIA A BORRELLI
VIA MANIN
VIA E ALBANESE
VIA ARCHIMEDE
VIA DALIA
VIA OMODEI
VIA E XIMENES
VIA EMPEDOCLE
VIA I CARINI
SELLA
CORSO D SCINÀ
VIA COLL DI S MARIA
VIA FRANCESCO CRISPI
VIA DEL MARE
VIA QUINTINO
VIA LA LUMIA
V TORREARSA
VIA N GALLO
PIAZZA STURZO
VIA EMERICO AMARI
VIA B GRAVINA
VIA AMMIRAGLIO GRAVINA
PRINCIPE
VIA M MIRAGLIA
VIA LA MASA
PIAZZA RUGGERO SETTIMO
VIA R WAGNER
VIA PRINCIPE DI BELMONTE
PRINCIPE GRANATELLI
STABILE
MARIANO
VIA ROMA
V FONDERIA ORETEA
VIA ONORATO
GUARDIONE
VIA RIOLO
VIA G FERRARIS
VIA VOLTA
VIA FILIPPO PATTI
VIA RUGGERO SETTIMO
VIA MARIANO STABILE
VIA VILLAERMOSA
VIA BENTIVEGNA
VIA CARELLA
VIA R PILO
VIA N COZZO
VIA C CAVOUR
VIA MAGLIOCCO
V SPERLUNGA
VIA SALVATORE SPINUZZA
VIA PIGNATELLI ARAGONA
La Zisa
Teatro Massimo
VIA BARA ALL' OLIVELLA
Museo Archeologico Regionale
PIAZZA OLIVELLA
Piazza delle Poste
Museo del Risorgimento
VIA VALVERDE
VIA SQUARCIALUPO
VIA CASTELLO
PIAZZA PANTELLERIA
VIA TAVOLA TONDA
VIA G MELI
VIA G BIVONA
VIA DELLA CALA
Museo Internazionale delle Marionette & Opera dei Pupi
Terrazza a Mare
FORO ITALICO
PIAZZA G VERDI
VIA ROSSINI
VIA DONIZETTI
VIA A AMICO
VIA MAQUEDA
VIA G PATANIA
V MONTELEONE
San Domenico
PIAZZA S DOMENICO
V MATERA
VIA CASSARI
Palazzo Chiaramonte
VIA BUTERA
VIA S GREGORIO
VIA FAVARA
VIA S AGOSTINO
VIA BANDIERA
VUCCIRIA
VIA NAPOLI
VIA VITTORIO EMANUELE
PIAZZA MARINA
IL CAPO
VIA PANNERIA
VIA VENEZIA
Sant'Antonio
VIA DEI BOTTAI
Palazzo Mirto
Galleria Regionale di Sicilia
VIA SCOPARI
VIA TORREMUZZA
PIAZZA DELLA KALSA
V D SEDIE VOLANTI
VIA JUDICA
VIA BEATI PAOLI
VIA DEI CANDELAI
SAL S ANTONIO
V ZARA
PIAZZA CASSA DI RISPARMIO
V MERLO
VIA PATERNOSTRO
LA KALSA
La Gancia
V GERVASI
Santa Teresa alla Kalsa
VIA GIOENI
V COLLEGIO GIUSINO
VIA DEL CELSO
VIA MONTEVERGINI
VIC MAROTTA
VIC RAGUSI
QUATTRO CANTI
Santa Caterina Church
VIA LUNGARINI
ALLORO
VIA DELLA VETRIERA
VIA SPASIMO
VIA N CERVELLO
PIAZZA PRETORIA
VIA S ANNA
VIA CASTROFILIPPO
VIA F RISO
Cattedrale
PIAZZA D SETT ANGELI
San Giuseppe dei Teatini
Church of Santa Maria Dell'Ammiraglio
VIA SCHIAVUZZO
Santa Maria dello Spasimo
Università
San Cataldo
VIA CALDERAI
PIAZZA DELLA RIVOLUZIONE
Palazzo Aiutamicristo
PIAZZA MAGIONE
La Magione
Villa Giulia
Palazzo Arcivescovile
PIAZZA ORIGLIONE
V G MUGLIA
VIA DIVISI
ALBERGHERIA
VIA ABRAMO LINCOLN
VIA GARIBALDI
VIA MAGIONE
VIA DELLA PACE
V FILANGERI
PIAZZA DELLA VITTORIA
VIA DEI BISCOTTARI
RUA FORMAGGI
VIA CASA PROFESSA
Chiesa del Gesu Professa
Palazzo Santa Croce
Orto Botanico
VIA BALLARO
VIC DEL BOSCO
VIA MILANO
PIAZZA M F BARONIO
VIA LUIGI CADORNA
VIA PORTA DI CASTRO
VIA A MONGITORE
VIA ALBERGHERIA
PIAZZA CARMINE
VIA D CASE NUOVE
VIA TORINO
VIA TRIESTE
PIAZZA GIULIO CESARE
VIA A DI RUDINI
VIA ANTONIO UGO
VIA ARCHIRAFI
VIA RANDAZZO
VIA M CIPOLLA
VIA G MIGNOSI
V G GRASSO
PORTA S AGATA
V CHIAPPARA AL CARMINE
VIA M DI S AGATA
VIA ROSSELLI
V G MAJALI
VIA VOLTO
CORSO TUKORY
Stazione Centrale
VIA R GREGORIO
V BALSAMO
V R PIRRI
CORSO DEI MILLE
San Giovanni degli Eremiti
VIA ALBERGHERIA
CRISTINA
VIA C FORLANINI
VIA DEL VESPRO
VIA C PISACANE
VIA P EMILIANI GIUDICI
VIA F P PEREZ
VIA ORETO
VIA A MARINUZZI
ERRANTE
VIA F FEDELE
PIAZZETTA CAIROLI
VIA FILICUZZA
VIA PIETRO D'ARAGONA
VIA M S SALAMONE
V GIORGIO ARCOLEO
VIA S BOCCONE
VIA TIRO A SEGNO
1
2
3
4
5
6
7
8
9
10
11
12
13
14
15
16

THE CITY

trees, their gigantic exposed roots spreading out across the grounds under towering palms. In the 10th century this was where jousting contests were held and executions performed. Nowadays pensioners gather here to pass the time playing cards and gossiping. This peaceful spot is surrounded by palaces, cafés and restaurants.

The largest palace on the square is the 14th-century **Palazzo Chiaramonte** (🕿 (091) 625 3892) on the east side of the piazza. The most interesting portion of the *palazzo* is the façade with its two tiers of windows surrounded by magnificent stone inlays. From 1685

VIA ROMA & THE VUCCIRIA

to 1782 the *palazzo* was the home of the Inquisition before it became the city's law courts. Today it is the administration building for the university and is only open to the public for special exhibitions.

Villa Giulia

Next door to the Orto Botanico is another peaceful oasis, the Villa Giulia. Created in 1778 and enlarged in 1866, the park bears the name of its patron, Giulia Avalos Guevara, the wife of the ruling

The grounds of the Villa Giulia are a peaceful haven in a busy city

THE CITY

PALAZZO MIRTO

When you emerge from a look around the stunning Palazzo Mirto, the chances are that you won't be blinking away too many tears at the economic plight of 17th-century Palermitan nobility. In fact you may well find yourself humming a few bars of the Communist anthem, *Bandiera Rossa*; for this stunning baroque palace, which was the seat of the wealthy Lanza Filangeri family (the last surviving member of which donated it to the Italian government in 1982), fair drips with decadent décor and fantastically fancy fixtures and fittings, chief among which – astonishingly – are many items from the original furnishings.

Before you enter the building, you'll get more than a hint of the luxury in which the financially unembarrassable immersed themselves, especially if you take a peek at the stables in which the Lanza Filangeris parked their steeds. Within lies an amazing collection of the most beautiful bronze horse-heads. When you consider that, in this society, stables were on a rough decorative par with the outside toilet, you get a clear idea of the outbuildings' design budget.

The first floor is the only portion of the palace that's open to the public, but interior design fans will probably still go into sensory overload, once they see the magnificent ceilings, the Chinese Room and the tapestries, all of which are still in excellent condition. Dotted around the rooms are items of exquisite cutlery and crockery, alongside such evocative bric-a-brac as the fans that society ladies would flutter when foppish beaux essayed a roguish comment. Atmospheric is hardly the word for the experience on offer here, indeed it's difficult not

VIA ROMA & THE VUCCIRIA

to be transported back to a 1750-vintage masked ball.
ⓐ Via Merlo 2 ⓣ (091) 616 7541 ⓛ 09.00–13.30 Mon, Wed, Fri & Sat, 09.30–13.30, 15.00–18.00 Tues, Thur, 09.00–13.00 Sun
ⓑ Bus: 101, 102, 103, 104, 107

● *Palazzo Mirto offers a rare chance to examine the original interior décor*

THE CITY

viceroy of the time. Covering the grounds are acres of aromatic flowers, a children's train, bandstand, deer and ducks. ❸ Via Abramo Lincoln ❶ (091) 740 4028 ❷ 08.00–20.00 ❹ Bus: 139, 211, 221, 224, 226, 227

CULTURE

Once you cross Via Vittorio Emanuele you will come to the church of Sant'Antonio. The stairs on the side of the church lead down to the Vucciria quarter, with its enormous marketplace, churches and museums.

Museo Archeologico Regionale

Although it could use a good dusting and it is not state-of-the-art, this is one of the grandest archaeological museums in Italy and well worth a visit.

The museum is stocked with artefacts dating from prehistoric times to the Roman era. Contained in several buildings, the oldest one from the 13th century, is an excellent collection of monumental Sicilian finds from Phoenician, Punic, Greek, Roman and Saracen periods.

Enter the ground floor through the smaller of two cloisters where you will find displays of anchors from the sea off the Sicilian coast. Another small room has Phoenician art, most notably a pair of sarcophagi dating to the 5th century BC. Beyond that is a room with Egyptian and Punic finds including the Pietra di Palermo, a black diorite slab known as the Rosetta Stone of Palermo (the other three parts of the Stone are in Cairo and London), dating back to 2700 BC. Etched on the stone in hieroglyphics is 700 years of Egyptian history. There is also a Punic one recovered from the harbour in Marsala with the figure of a priest worshipping the god Tanit.

VIA ROMA & THE VUCCIRIA

Further along the cloister is dedicated to Roman sculpture, on the left is Emperor Claudius enthroned in the style of Zeus. Other rooms showcase early Greek-carved *stelae* and several inscribed tablets. Beyond here the exhibits are mostly of Greek origin, the stone lion's-head water spouts from the Victory Temple at Himera, 5th century BC.

The most important collection of the museum is the Sala di Selinunte, unique stone carvings (metopes) from Temples A–G at Selinunte on the southwest coast. The friezes were used to adorn the temples and show mythological scenes. The earliest friezes are from the 6th century BC, the panels depict the gods of Delphi, the Sphinx, the rape of Europa, and Hercules and the Bull. The most vivid panels, such as *Perseus Beheading Medusa* (his head and torso pointing directly out at you), date back to the 5th century BC and were unearthed from Temples C and F.

Also on exhibit are panels from the early 5th century BC Temple E. They portray Hercules battling an Amazon, the marriage of Zeus and Hera, Actaeon being savaged by dogs, and Athena and the Titan.

Retrace your steps to the small cloister for the stairs up to the first floor where you will find many other exhibits of interest, among them lead water pipes retrieved from an archaeological site at Termini Imerese (now Therma Himeraia) – originally settled by Greeks in the 7th century BC, it is still famous for its healing waters. Also on display are more than 12,000 votive terracotta figures and some carved stone heads found at Solunto, a place that had been settled by the Phoenicians in the 8th century BC, and then later by the Greeks who surrendered it to the Romans during the First Punic War.

The second floor of the museum is not to be missed as it is here that there is a room full of splendidly preserved Roman mosaics. The

THE CITY

largest, measuring 10 m (33 ft) in length, was excavated from Piazza della Vittoria in Palermo. The *Triumph of Neptune* mosaic dates from the 2nd century AD, while another from the 3rd century AD shows Orpheus with a lyre surrounded by friendly beasts. ⓐ Piazza Olivella 24 ⓘ (091) 611 6805 ⓛ 08.30–18.00 Tues–Sat, 09.00–13.00 Sun, closed Mon ⓝ Bus: 101, 102, 103, 104, 107

Museo del Risorgimento

The buildings adjacent to the church of San Domenico belong to the Sicilian Historical Society (Societa Siciliana per la Storia Patria) with the small (but interesting) Museo del Risorgimento, which has an excellent collection of exhibits pertaining to the 19th-century Italian anti-Bourbon revolt, and containing mementoes of Garibaldi. Adjacent to the museum are some beautiful 14th-century cloisters. ⓐ Piazza San Domenico 1 ⓘ (091) 329 588 ⓛ 09.00–13.00 Mon, Wed, Fri, closed Sat & Sun, Tues, Thur; ring for entry ⓝ Bus: 101

Palace of La Zisa

West of the centre of Palermo is the palace of La Zisa. Taken from the Arabic *al-aziz* or 'the magnificent', this towering palace was built in North African style, as a king's retreat. At one time it was stocked with beautifully laid out gardens and rare and exotic beasts. The palace languished for centuries within a large private estate and, today, is surrounded by blocks of modern apartments. But, the good news is that La Zisa has been mostly restored and displayed within it are wonderful Islamic mosaic designs, a large collection of Islamic art and artefacts. ⓐ Piazza Gugliemo il Buono (near Piazza Camporeale, at the end of Via Dante) ⓘ (091) 652 0269 ⓛ 09.00–19.00 Mon–Sat, closed Sun ⓝ Bus: 124 from Piazza Politeama. Admission charge

VIA ROMA & THE VUCCIRIA

La Zisa, from Arabic al-aziz *(the magnificent), is a stunning building*

Piazza delle Poste

The huge, concrete, chunky building on the left of Via Roma is Piazza delle Poste, built by the Fascists in 1933. Today it is Palermo's main post office. The only good thing about the building is the pink colour of the exterior walls, which softens the blow of looking at it and lends a nice hue at night when the building is lit. Around the corner from this hulk is the Piazza Olivella and the church of **Sant'Ignazio**

THE CITY

VIA ROMA & THE VUCCIRIA

Martire all'Olivella, with its elegant baroque interior. ⓐ Piazza Olivella ⓝ Bus: 101, 102, 103, 104, 107

San Domenico

On the north side of the marketplace is San Domenico, an extraordinary 18th-century church. The baroque façade rises in three ordered tiers of Doric and Corinthian columns and square pilasters framing the statue of St Domenic. The enormous interior is separated into aisles and the nave, with a chapel off each bay and holds tombs of famous Sicilian painters, poets and writers. The church is an impressive sight at night when the entire front is lit. ⓐ Piazza San Domenico ⓣ (091) 584 872 ⓛ 09.00–11.30 Mon–Fri, 17.00–19.00 Sat & Sun ⓝ Bus: 101

RETAIL THERAPY

If you want high-end fashion this is not the quarter for it – head over to Via della Libertà and Via Principe di Belmonte. What you will find in the Via Roma and Vucciria quarter is a marketplace full of stalls selling fish, vegetables and pastry along with housewares, shoes and clothing. The narrow streets surrounding the quarter have a few shops offering some unique goods.

Emporio Bucalo A clothing store where men will find the most refined shirts and clothing items. There are many stores throughout the city, so it will be easy to locate. ⓐ Via Ugo La Malfa 15 ⓣ (091) 685 2854 ⓦ www.bucalo1987.it ⓛ 09.00–13.00, 15.30–19.00 Mon–Fri, 09.00–13.00, 16.00–20.00 Sat, closed Sun ⓝ Bus: 116, 105

◀ *Relax in the Orto Botanico and enjoy the exotic specimen plants*

THE CITY

Giuseppe Gramuglia A paradise for those who like to do something flamboyant with a bit of fabric, this shop has mountains of the stuff, in all its forms. ⓐ Via Roma 412–414 (corner of Via Principe di Belmonte) ⓣ (091) 583 262 ⓞ 09.00–13.00, 15.30–19.00 Mon–Fri, 09.00–13.00, 16.00–20.00 Sat, closed Sun Ⓝ Bus: 104, 107, 122, 124, 224, 225

Postolato Liturgico Staffed by white-clad nuns, the shop specialises in church-related finery. Glass cabinets hold gold chalices and medallions, many of them encrusted with gemstones, and stunning liturgical robes. ⓐ Via Vittorio Emanuele 454 ⓣ (091) 651 2467 ⓞ 09.00–13.00, 15.30–19.00 Mon–Fri, 09.00–13.00, 16.00–20.00 Sat, closed Sun Ⓝ Bus: 103, 104, 105, 108, 110, 118

TAKING A BREAK

Cana Wine Bar £ ❶ Located in a medieval building behind Piazza Marina, this charming intimate wine bar, open only in the evenings, is an ideal spot for an aperitif after a day of exploring. ⓐ Via Alloro 105 ⓣ (091) 610 1147 ⓞ 19.00–23.00 Ⓝ Bus: 101, 103, 104, 107

La Corrida £ ❷ Located in a row of bars across from the archaeological museum. Good for a snack and a rest. ⓐ Piazza Olivella 9 ⓞ 15.00–23.30 Ⓝ Bus: 101, 102, 103, 104, 107

Ilardo £ ❸ Ice cream is a passion in Palermo, and the Ilardo – which has been in business for decades – is known for its excellent ice cream. ⓐ Foro Italico 12 (at the end of Via Alloro) ⓞ 15.00–23.00 Ⓝ Bus: 101, 103, 104, 107

VIA ROMA & THE VUCCIRIA

Renna's Self Serve £ ❹ Simple caféteria-style restaurant, good for an informal lunch or dinner or if you are in a hurry. Nothing fancy, just delicious Italian food at reasonable prices. ⓐ Off Via Roma near the Hotel delle Palme ⓛ 12.00–14.00, 19.00–22.30 ⓝ Bus: 104, 107, 122, 124, 224, 225

Tabuca £ ❺ A cosy, quiet little spot great place to relax with a glass of wine and people-watch. ⓐ Piazza Marina 6 ⓛ 15.00–23.00 ⓝ Bus: 101, 102, 103, 104, 107

AFTER DARK

The Piazza Marina is ringed with restaurants and cafés as are many of the churches, narrow streets and alleys in this area. You'll find other listings nearby in the La Kalsa chapter (see page 108).

Antica Focacceria San Francesco £ ❻ An old-time *pizzeria* that must be doing something right because it has been open since 1834. Great, inexpensive pizzas. ⓐ Via A. Paternostro 59 (off Via Vittorio Emanuele and opposite the church of San Francesco) ⓣ (091) 320 264 ⓦ www.anticafocacceriasanfrancesco.it ⓛ 10.00–00.00 ⓝ Bus: 103, 105, 225

La Traviata £ ❼ Tucked away in a quiet alley, steps from the Museo Archeologico. The pasta choices are excellent and inexpensive. ⓐ Piazza Olivella 18 ⓛ 19.00–00.00 ⓝ Bus: 101, 102, 103, 104, 107

Il Cantastorie ££ ❽ Close to the beach and run by the seafaring Marino family, Il Cantastorie offers a tempting range of seafood as well as pizzas. ⓐ Via Messina Marine 166 ⓣ (091) 621 1121

W www.marinoilcantastorie.it ⏰ 12.00–15.00, 19.00–00.30 Tues–Sun, closed Mon 🚌 Bus: 221, 224, 225

Cucina Papoff ££ ❾ If you enjoy the food at this friendly restaurant, you can find recipes for several of their dishes on their website. The *gnocchi* with gorgonzola are particularly tempting. 🏠 Via Isidoro La Lumia 32 📞 (091) 586 460 W www.cucinapapoff.com ⏰ 12.00–15.00, 19.00–00.30 Mon–Fri, 19.00–00.30 Sat, closed Sun 🚌 Bus: 101, 102, 104, 108

Il Mirto e la Rosa ££ ❿ The aromas of North African-prepared vegetable couscous and spicy pasta dishes are heady in this well-run establishment. Reservations recommended. 🏠 Via Principe di Granatelli 30 📞 (091) 324 353 ⏰ 13.00–15.00, 19.00–23.00 Tues–Sun, closed Mon, one week Aug 🚌 Bus: 101, 102, 103

Trattoria Stella ££ ⓫ Although the sign over the door reads 'Hotel Patria', the hotel is no longer there but the excellent restaurant is. Specialities consist of barbecued lamb and fish dishes. Dine under the stars in the elegant medieval courtyard. 🏠 Via Alloro 104 (corner of Via Aragona) 📞 (091) 616 1136 ⏰ 13.00–15.00, 19.00–23.00 Tues–Sun, closed Mon 🚌 Bus: 101, 102

La Cambusa £££ ⓬ This elegant, quiet restaurant overlooking Piazza Marina specialises in fish dishes. There's also an excellent *antipasti* buffet. Menu prices do not include the restaurant's ten per cent service charge. 🏠 Piazza Marina 16 📞 (091) 584 574 W www.lacambusa.it ⏰ 12.00–15.00, 19.00–23.00 Tues–Sun, closed Mon 🚌 Bus: 103, 105, 225

VIA ROMA & THE VUCCIRIA

Kursaal Tonnara £££ ⓑ A complex of two restaurants, two bars, and an open-air theatre occupy this beautiful 15th-century structure, previously a tuna fishing plant. Reservations are recommended.
ⓐ Via Bordonaro 9 ⓣ (091) 637 2267 ⓦ www.kursaaltonnara.it
ⓛ 19.00–00.30 Wed–Mon, closed Tues ⓝ Bus: 139, 603, 731

Ristorante Cin Cin £££ ⓫ As well as a varied menu, this pleasant restaurant offers cookery classes, including a trip to the local markets (the classes require advance booking). ⓐ Via Manin 22
ⓣ (091) 612 4095 ⓦ www.ristorantecincin.com ⓛ 19.00–00.30
ⓝ Bus: 102, 103, 118

Trattoria a Cuccagna £££ ⓯ Run by a father and son team, A Cuccagna can boast Tom Cruise and Francis Ford Coppola among their customers. ⓐ Via Principe di Granatelli 21a ⓣ (091) 587 267
ⓦ www.acuccagna.com ⓛ 12.00–15.00, 19.00–00.30 ⓝ Bus: 101, 102, 103

Sant'Andrea £££+ ⓰ This stylish restaurant is the reason you brought that chic black dress or that suit and tie. Located near the Piazza San Domenico and the Vucciria market where most of the restaurants ingredients come from; they don't have menus, the delicious creations are at the whim of the chef. The fantastic desserts are made on the premises, and there's a superior wine list. Reserve well in advance for an outside table. ⓐ Piazza Sant'Andrea 4
ⓣ (091) 334 999 ⓛ 19.30–00.30 Wed–Mon, closed Tues, Jan ⓝ Bus: 101, 103, 104, 107

THE CITY

La Kalsa – the Historic Quarter

'Balarm, the immense city of beauty, the wondrous splendid sojourn, the world's vast metropolis, adorned in elegance… Balarm has buildings of such beauty that travellers come from afar to the well-known marvels of its architecture.' Al Idrisi (1099–1166).

The 'Balarm' that Muslim geographer Al Idrisi refers to in this quote is Palermo. It was written at the time when La Kalsa, from Arabic *khalisa* (meaning pure), was the city's cultural and intellectual centre. Al Idrisi was the court geographer to the Emir of Sicily, which was under Arab rule before King Roger ascended the throne.

Al Idrisi's knowledge and competence caught the attention of Roger II, the Norman King, who invited him to produce an up-to-date world map. He constructed a circular map of pure silver that weighed 400 kilograms (880 lbs) and precisely recorded on it the seven continents with trade routes, lakes and rivers, major cities, and plains and mountains. Al Idrisi described the world in *Al-Kitab al-Rujari* (*Roger's Book*), also entitled *Nuzhat al-Mushtag fi Ikhtirag al-Afag* (*The Delight of Him Who Desires to Journey Through the Climates*). He spent most of his life in service to King Roger II.

Designed and built by the Saracens, La Kalsa is one of Palermo's oldest quarters. It lies behind the port and was heavily bombed in 1943, when many people were killed and countless buildings destroyed. The ruins were thrown into the sea and, as a result, the Foro Italico, a short distance from the seafront, was created with the rubble.

Today, there is still more work to be done, but almost the entire district has undergone a complete restoration. New squares have been created, one of which is Piazza Magione, laid out like an English meadow, the *palazzi* and monuments have been dusted and cleaned and cultural centres such as Santa Maria dello Spasimo (see page 104)

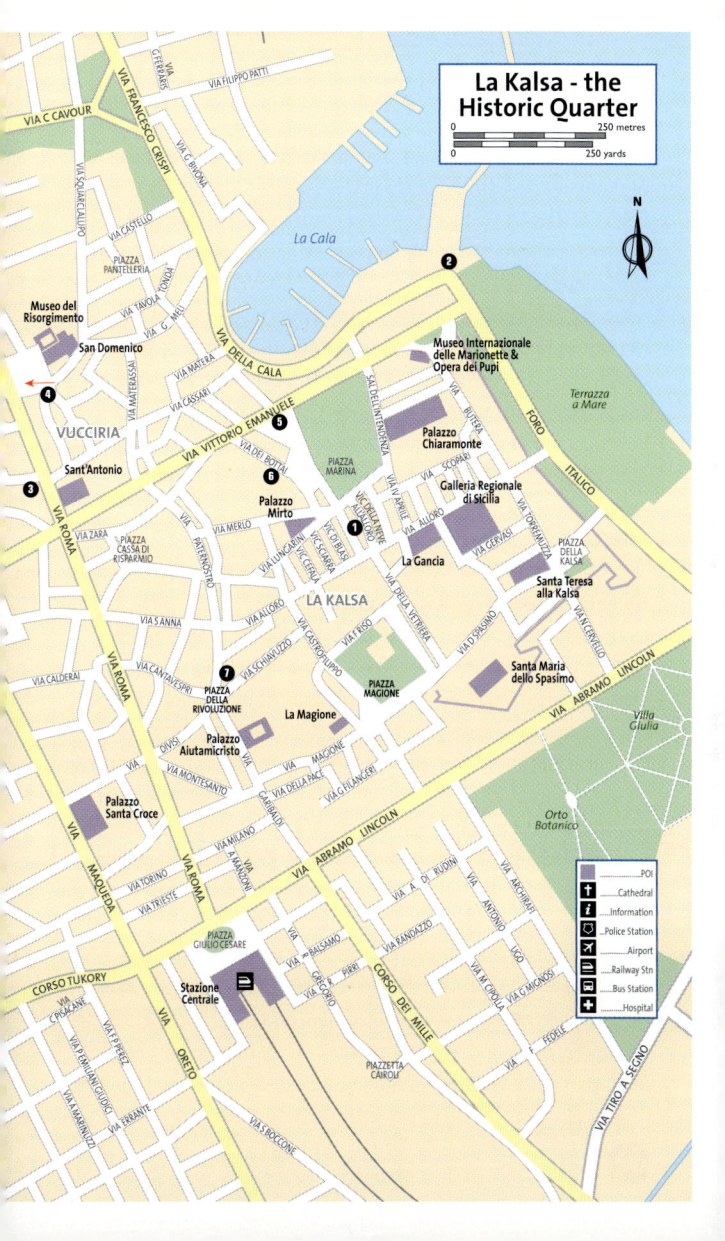

La Kalsa - the Historic Quarter

0 — 250 metres
0 — 250 yards

N

La Cala

VIA C CAVOUR
VIA FRANCESCO CRISPI
VIA CETRARO
VIA FILIPPO PATTI
VIA C ROMA
VIA SQUARCIALUPO
VIA CASTELLO
PIAZZA PANTELLERIA
VIA TAVOLA TONDA
VIA G MELI

Museo del Risorgimento
San Domenico
VIA DELLA CALA
VIA MATRASSI
VIA CASSARI
VUCCIRIA
Sant'Antonio
VIA VITTORIO EMANUELE
VIA DEI BOTTAI
Museo Internazionale delle Marionette & Opera dei Pupi
SAL DI INTENDENZA
VIA BUTERA
FORO ITALICO
Terrazza a Mare
Palazzo Chiaramonte
PIAZZA MARINA
VIA SCOPARI
VIA ZARA
VIA ROMA
Palazzo Mirto
VIA MERLO
VIA LUNGARINI
VIA SC GEMMA
VIA CERDA
VIA PATERNOSTRO
PIAZZA CASSA DI RISPARMIO
Galleria Regionale di Sicilia
VIA ALLORO
La Gancia
VIA GERVASI
PIAZZA DELLA KALSA
Santa Teresa alla Kalsa
VIA DELLA VETRIERA
VIA D SPASIMO
VIA N CERVELLO
LA KALSA
VIA S ANNA
VIA ALLORO
VIA CANTAVESPRI
VIA CASTROFILIPPO
VIA FICO
Santa Maria dello Spasimo
PIAZZA DELLA RIVOLUZIONE
VIA SCHIOPPETTIERI
PIAZZA MAGIONE
VIA ABRAMO LINCOLN
Villa Giulia
VIA CALDERAI
VIA ROMA
La Magione
Palazzo Aiutamicristo
VIA DIVISI
VIA MONTESANTO
VIA MAGIONE
VIA DELLA PACE
VIA CARDUCCI
VIA G FLANGERI
Orto Botanico
Palazzo Santa Croce
VIA MILANO
VIA ROMA
VIA MAQUEDA
VIA TORINO
VIA TRIESTE
VIA RANDONI
VIA ABRAMO LINCOLN
VIA A. DI RUDINI
VIA ANTONIO UGO
VIA ARCHIRAFI
PIAZZA GIULIO CESARE
VIA RANDAZZO
VIA N BALSAMO
CORSO DEI MILLE
VIA M CURIA
VIA G MIGNOSI
CORSO TUKORY
VIA CIPRIANO
VIA PAPPARI
VIA FABIANI GIUDICI
VIA MARINUZZI
VIA ORETO
Stazione Centrale
VIA L ORO
VIA GR PIERI
VIA M FEDELE
VIA ERRANTE
PIAZZETTA CAIROLI
VIA S BOCCONE
VIA TIRO A SEGNO

Legend:
- POI
- Cathedral
- Information
- Police Station
- Airport
- Railway Stn
- Bus Station
- Hospital

THE CITY

host numerous concerts year round of jazz and classical music, many of them free. From mid-June to mid-September the quarter is jumping with the KalsArt Festival (see page 10), a cultural extravaganza of live music, theatre and cinema events that take place throughout the La Kalsa district.

La Kalsa is bounded rather neatly by Via Vittorio Emanuele to the north, Foro Italico to the east, Via Abramo Lincoln to the south and Via Roma to the west. Via Sanna and Via Alloro join together to cut it in half horizontally. The heart of the quarter is Piazza della Kalsa, containing many of the city's most interesting Arab-Norman architecture, monuments, museums, parks and churches.

CULTURE

Galleria Regionale di Sicilia (Regional Gallery)

Housed in the 15th-century Palazzo Abatellis, and designed by Matteo Carnelivari in 1490, is the Galleria Regionale, with its brilliant medieval art collection. The *palazzo* holds its own among all the brilliance of the inside art, though it still retains elements of its Catalan-Gothic and Renaissance origin in its doorway and courtyard. Heavily damaged in the World War II bombings, its interior was restored in 1954 by Carlo Scarpa, one of Italy's foremost contemporary interior designers. For each important work of art contained here, Scarpa used different materials and colours to display the art in the best possible way and enhance the natural daylight to the fullest.

The museum has 16 exhibition rooms, which alternatively display paintings and sculpture masterpieces by artists Francesco Laurana, Antonello da Messina, Antonello Gagini and his school, Domenico Gagini, Serpotta and others. Laurana's white marble bust of the Spanish infanta Eleonora of Aragon, a study in peace and tranquillity,

LA KALSA – THE HISTORIC QUARTER

> **THE OLD HARBOUR – LA CALA**
> The thumb-shaped inlet of the old city harbour, La Cala, was once Palermo's main port. Its unfortunate decline started in the 16th century, when silting caused the water to recede to its current position. The fishermen and trade ships moved northwest to docks off what is now Stazione Marittima. Today La Cala's primary function is as marina to the yachts of the well-heeled. The docks are great for a stroll around, and to enjoy the excellent views over the little harbour to Monte Pellegrino in the distance.

can be found on the ground floor in room 4. Room 5 is devoted to works by the noted Gagini's, a particular eye-catcher being Antonello Gagini's *Archangel Michael*.

The back wall of room 2 has the magnificent 15th-century fresco, the *Triumph of Death*. This chilling study casts a cruel and realistic figure of Death as an archer sitting astride a galloping, skeletal horse, trampling people who are in the full blush of youth, and whom he has slain with his arrows. It hauntingly depicts the facial expressions of the old and sick as they plead hopelessly for oblivion as Death ignores them and rides towards a group of wealthy citizens who are apparently unconcerned by his approach. Formerly attributed to a Catalan painter, the fresco is now regarded as a Gothic work and is attributed to the school of Pisanello, Veronese Antonio Pisano, known as Pisanello as he was the son of a Pisan draper.

Of the excellent 15th-century Sicilian art on this floor, the most notable work is by Antonello da Messina, the ethereal *Our Lady of the Annunciation*; painted in 1473 it is considered to be one of

THE CITY

da Messina's finest works. The brightness of the colours, the blue of the mantle, the pale brown of the complexion, the yellow of the pulpit, is remarkable. The purity of the Virgin's oval face is enhanced by the mantle framing it.

The masterpiece *Malvagna Triptych* by Dutch painter Jan Gossaert (known as Mabuse), covers an entire wall. The Malvagna, painted in 1510, depicts the Virgin enthroned with Child and angels. ⓐ Palazzo Abatellis, Via Alloro 4 ⓘ (091) 623 0011 ⓛ 09.00–13.30 Fri–Mon, 09.00–13.30, 14.30–19.30 Tues–Thur Ⓝ Bus: 103, 105, 139 or the Linea Gialla (yellow line). Admission charge

La Gancia

The 15th-century church of La Gancia, or Santa Maria degli Angeli, next to the Galleria Regionale di Sicilia, has more works of art by the Gagini family in the way of sculpted fragments and reliefs. Built by the Franciscans in the late 1400s, the church has undergone numerous alterations that have modified its appearance, most particularly on the interior. Remaining of the original exterior are the square profile and rustication.

The church's baroque interior is worth a visit to view the magnificent late-1500s organ by Raffaele della Valle. ⓐ Via Alloro 27 ⓘ (091) 616 5221 ⓛ 09.30–12.00, 15.00–18.00 Mon–Sat, 10.00–12.30 Sun Ⓝ Bus: 103, 105, 139 or the Linea Gialla (yellow line)

Museo Internazionale delle Marionette

On the harbour side of the quarter, near Foro Italico, you will find the Museo delle Marionette. The museum is devoted to puppets of all kinds, the Sicilian *pupi*, puppets based on characters from the French *chansons de geste*, marionettes, articulated puppets operated with strings, shadow puppets and Punch and Judy in their traditional

booth. Via Butera 1, near Piazzetta Niscemi (091) 328 060
www.museomarionettepalermo.it 09.00–13.00, 16.00–19.00
Mon–Fri, closed Sat & Sun Bus: 103, 105, 139, 225. Admission charge

Opera dei Pupi (Puppet Theatre)
Opera dei Pupi, or Puppet Theatre, embodies a strong sense of Palermo's culture, so much so that in 2001 it was declared a masterpiece of oral tradition by UNESCO.

Palermo's tradition of puppetry lives on at Opera dei Pupi

THE CITY

The marionette tradition dates back to the 16th century. These masterpiece creations, many of which are hundreds of years old, are brightly painted and costumed puppets made of wood and controlled by a wire attached to the head and right hand of each puppet. A dying art across the rest of the island, Palermo's puppet theatre is still going strong and much beloved.

The puppet masters tell stories of bandits, romance, heroism, duels and of course feature Punch and Judy in their traditional setting. This is not to be missed and is great fun for all age groups.

Puppet Theatre tourist performances are held at the Museo Internazionale delle Marionette (see page 100). ❸ Vicolo Niscemi 5 ❶ (091) 328 060 ❷ 09.00–13.00, 15.00–18.30 Mon–Fri, 09.00–13.00 Sat, closed Sun and public holidays. Admission charge

Piazza Magione and its surroundings

The church of **La Magione** (❸ Via Magione ❶ (091) 617 0596) stands at the end of the palm-shaded lane of Piazza Maggiore. This excellent example of Arab-Norman architecture was built in 1151 for the Cistercians. In 1197 Henry IV gave it to the Order of the Teutonic knights for use as their headquarters. It remained in the knights hands for over 300 years.

The church was heavily damaged during World War II, but the cloisters were spared and their treasures are phenomenal. There is a Judaic tombstone re-carved into a marble holy water receptacle. In the room between the cloister and chapel is a fresco of the crucifixion and opposite it is a rare plaster interpretation of the fresco, the only existing example of a fresco model in Sicily. It shows the great detail and planning that went into the work. Alongside this is a small Arab-Norman column carved with a Koranic inscription in Kufic Arabic, a first-millennium angular script used

LA KALSA – THE HISTORIC QUARTER

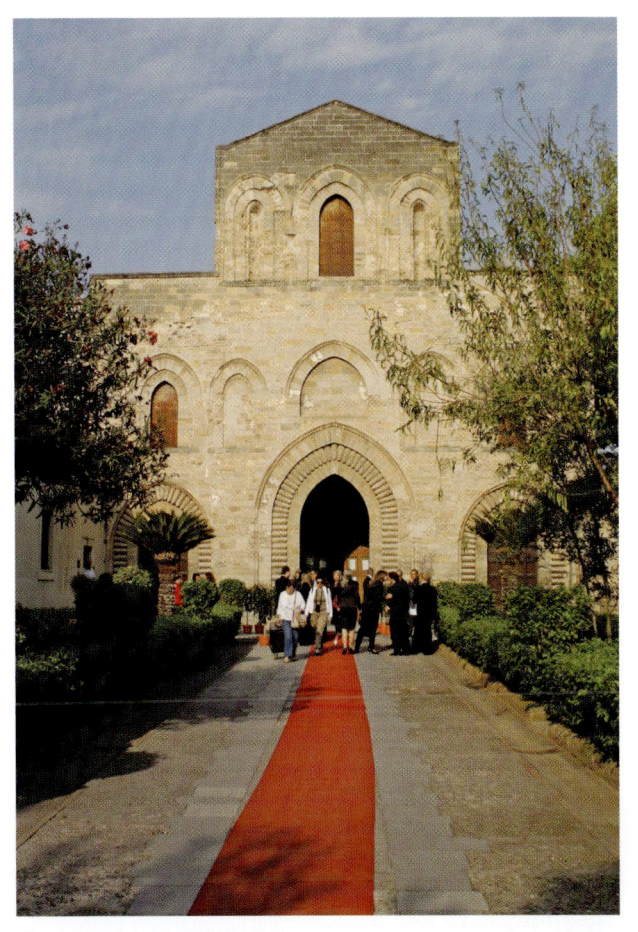

La Magione in the Kalsa

THE CITY

for inscribing on hard surfaces and extant throughout much early Islamic art.

The walls are lined with before and after photographs showing the façade of the church before it was restored to its original Arab-Norman design in the early 1900s.

Returning to Piazza Magione you will find an idyllic park that is a popular spot with Palermo's young set. It is a good spot to sit and relax.

Piazza della Rivoluzione

It was from here, in 1848, that the anti-Bourbon uprising began. In the centre of this pretty little piazza is an elaborate fountain depicting a king feeding a serpent.

From this piazza Via Garibaldi leads south, marking the end of the route that Garibaldi took in May 1860 when he entered the city marching north up Corso dei Mille and into what is now Via Garibaldi. **Palazzo Aiutamicristo** (❶ (091) 324 006), one of the largest 15th-century palaces designed by Matteo Carnelivari, is at Via Garibaldi 23.

Santa Maria dello Spasimo

Built inside the walls of the Kalsa in 1506, this church and convent were the work of Giacomo Basilico. It was Basilico who commissioned Raphael to paint *Lo Spasimo di Sicilia*, which was installed here in 1520 but is now in the Prado Museum in Madrid.

Building the church was a painstakingly slow process, it was not completed when the threat of war with Turkey made it necessary to build a Spanish bastion behind the church. Afterwards the complex was transformed into a fortress, then a theatre, in 1624 it became a hospice for plague victims, and finally a hospital for prostitutes. It was abandoned in 1986. The church and hospital have been restored and now are venues for cultural events.

LA KALSA – THE HISTORIC QUARTER

Accessible to the public is the area around the 16th-century cloisters, endowed with simple, elegant lines. Beyond these is the church, an excellent example of Catalan-Gothic style. The interior consists of three naves, with a tall slender nave reaching up towards the roofless top and the open sky, and ending with a gorgeous multilateral apse.

The original entrance walls contain two side chapels. The one on the left, with the rounded dome, gives access to the bastion, which is now a lovely garden. ⓐ Via dello Spasimo ⓣ (091) 616 6480 ⓛ Variable, depending on the event being staged, so phone to check ⓝ Bus: 103, 105, 139

Santa Teresa alla Kalsa

Beyond the entrance to the quarter, the Porta dei Greci, lies the Piazza della Kalsa and church of Santa Teresa alla Kalsa, a magnificent baroque church that took architect Paolo Amato 20 years (1686–1706) to complete. In the commanding façade are two orders of Corinthian columns, a monumental feat for the time in which the church was built. ⓐ Piazza della Kalsa ⓣ (091) 617 1658 ⓛ 09.00–20.00 ⓝ Bus: 103, 105, 139

Via Alloro

Via Alloro was La Kalsa's main street in the Middle Ages. Head west along it for a close-up view of this decaying district that lost many beautiful *palazzi* and is still under repair from the 1943 bombings.

RETAIL THERAPY

La Kalsa district's narrow streets are full of tiny shops that specialise in jewellery, liqueurs, silver, books and embroidery. The high fashion

THE CITY

shops, as mentioned before, are in the area around Via della Libertà. And, of course, there are the street markets. The closest ones to La Kalsa are the Vucciria at Piazza San Domenico and the Ballaro in the Albergheria district at Piazza Casa Professa.

Fecarotta One of Italy's oldest jewellers. Collections include antiques and modern pieces designed by famous designers. If you have a thing about bling, this is the shop for you. ⓐ Via Ruggero Settimo 68 ⓘ (091) 586 282 ⓛ 09.00–13.00, 16.00–20.00 Mon–Sat, closed Sun Ⓝ Bus: 104, 107

Tre Erre Ceramiche This shop is one of the most important and respected ceramic stores in Palermo. Here you will find high-quality pieces that will make a perfect gift to bring home. ⓐ Via E Amari 47 ⓘ (091) 323 827 ⓦ www.treerreceramiche.com ⓛ 09.00–13.00, 15.30–19.30 Mon–Sat (winter); 09.00–13.00, 16.00–20.00 Mon–Sat (summer), closed Sun Ⓝ Bus: 106, 107, 108

Tutone Since 1813 the Tutone family has been providing Palermitans and visitors with a traditional drink that dates back to the Arabs, Anise Unico, water flavoured with aniseed. Along with this refreshing pick-me-up the shop also carries lovely decanters of liqueurs and aperitifs. ⓐ Via Garibaldi 41 ⓘ (091) 616 1280 ⓦ www.tutone.it ⓛ 09.00–13.00, 15.30–19.00 Mon–Fri, 09.00–13.00, 16.00–20.00 Sat, closed Sun Ⓝ Bus: 103, 105, 139

TAKING A BREAK

Around Piazza della Kalsa indulge yourself with a delicious treat called *babbaluci* – baby snails. The aroma of the snails marinating

LA KALSA – THE HISTORIC QUARTER

in a mixture of olive oil, chopped parsley, garlic and red pepper permeates the air. Vendors sell them in paper cones called cornets. Take a noontime break under a tree or on a bench and enjoy.

Parco Culturale del Gattopardo £ ❶ This cultural centre and wine bar dedicated to the Sicilian author Giuseppe Tomasi di Lampedusa has an excellent wine list, and also offers *antipasti*, *panini* and good *granita*. There is a lovely cobbled terrace that's perfect for relaxing with a glass of Sicilian wine. ⓐ Vicolo della Neve all'Alloro ⓣ (091) 616 0796 ⓦ www.parcotomasi.it ⓛ 10.00–23.00 (summer); 10.00–15.00, 18.00–23.00 Wed–Mon, closed Tues (winter) ⓝ Bus: 103, 105

Kursaal Kalhesa £–££ ❷ A great place to meet young locals, most of whom are fluent in English. With its prime location in a restored palace near Piazza Marina, this is where Palermo meets New York SoHo. Read English-language newspapers, listen to live entertainment, go on-line at the internet café, or pick up tourist information at the travel agency. The upstairs restaurant serves Sicilian and Tunisian house specialities of artichoke pasta with a *radicchio* cream sauce, lemon-flavoured swordfish with shrimp and a local delicacy, lentils grown on the island of Ustica and flavoured with squid ink. ⓐ Foro Umberto 1 ⓣ (091) 616 7630 ⓛ 11.30–01.30 Tues–Sat, 11.30–18.30 Sun, closed Mon ⓝ Bus: 139, 221, 225, 250

AFTER DARK

La Kalsa is just as dangerous as it is fascinating. Keep your wits about you at all times. It's relatively safe during the day, but at night the labyrinthine streets are dark and it is best to take a taxi.

THE CITY

Ferro Di Cavallo £ ❸ Low prices and mouthwatering food characterise this friendly local *trattoria*. ⓐ Via Venezia 20 ⓣ (091) 331 835 ⓛ 12.00–15.00 Mon–Wed, 12.00–15.00, 20.00–01.00 Thur–Sat, closed Sun ⓝ Bus: 101, 102, 104, 107

Cambio Cavalli ££ ❹ A converted stable yard provides the charming setting for this restaurant. ⓐ Via Patania 54 ⓣ (091) 581 418 ⓦ www.cambiocavalli.com ⓛ 12.00–15.00, 20.00–00.00 Tues–Sun, closed Mon ⓝ Bus: 102, 104

La Pergamène ££ ❺ Pizza and seafood are the order of the day at this pleasant al fresco restaurant. For other restaurants around Piazza Marina see page 93. ⓐ Piazza Marina 48–49 ⓣ (091) 616 6142 ⓛ 19.00–00.00 Tues–Sun, closed Mon ⓝ Bus: 101, 102, 104, 107

Lo Scalino del Cardinale ££ ❻ Specialities of this elegant restaurant include *caponata* (a vegetarian dish made with aubergine) and *stigghiole* (a kebab made with lamb). ⓐ Via dei Bottai 18 ⓣ (091) 331 124 ⓦ www.loscalinodelcardinale.net ⓛ 12.00–15.00, 19.00–00.00 ⓝ Bus: 101, 102, 104, 107

Trattoria Al Genio ££ ❼ Small, family-run *trattoria* offering good seafood and grilled meats. ⓐ Piazza San Carlo 9 (Piazza Rivoluzione) ⓣ (091) 616 6142 ⓛ 12.00–15.00, 20.00–00.00, Wed–Mon, closed Tues ⓝ Bus: 103, 105,

▶ *Explore the narrow streets of Monreale*

OUT OF TOWN
trips

OUT OF TOWN

Mondello

When the summer sun burns hot, when old men on the square seek a place in the shade and when children tire of seeing churches and monuments, head for the beach. For Palermo residents and visitors alike that means the beach of the small fishing village of Mondello. At one time Mondello was a snobbish retreat for the Sicilian upper crust, evoking the most fashionable parts of the French Riviera. After World War II it more democratically became a 'beach for everyone', and now it can get crowded during the summer.

GETTING THERE

Mondello is only 11 km (7 miles) from Palermo (see map, page 112), so you can take a trip there and always be within easy and quick reach of the city centre.

By road
Regular bus services make the half-hour trip from Palermo to Mondello. From Piazza Sturzo or Via della Libertà in Palermo, take bus number 806, and in summer number 833 also runs to the resort. The last bus leaves Mondello about 23.30. A taxi back to the city centre costs approximately €30.

SIGHTS & ATTRACTIONS

Mondello Beach
Mondello's marvellous sandy beach stretches 2 km (1 mile) and opens onto a half-moon shaped bay between Monte Pellegrino and Monte Gallo. For centuries, it has lured not only fishermen to

MONDELLO

🔺 *Mondello attracts sunbathers and sailors alike*

OUT OF TOWN

AROUND PALERMO

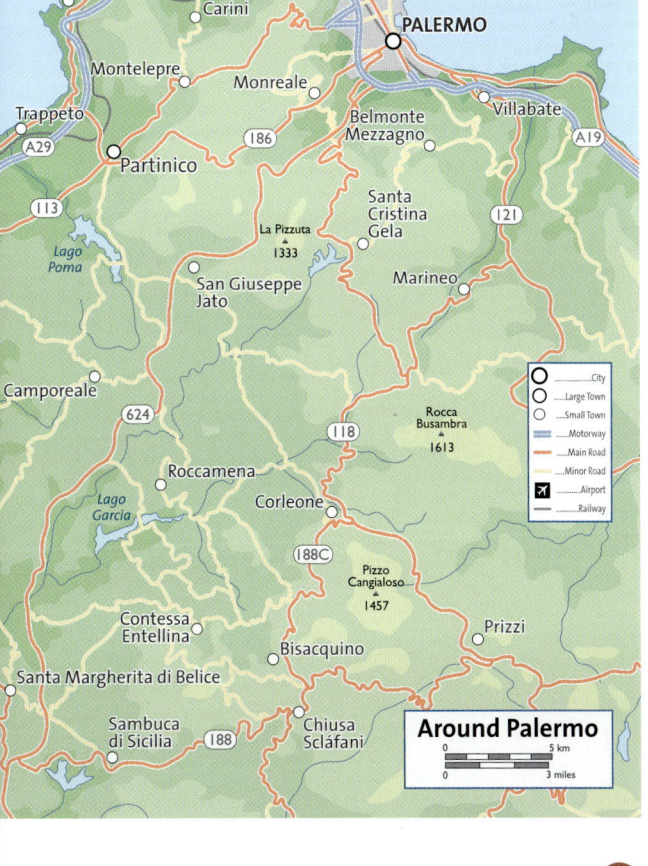

OUT OF TOWN

its harbour full of fish, mussels, clams and octopus, but also visitors and Sicilians alike. The beach, or lido, leads up to the town with its hotels, bars, cafés and nightclubs. Come in the daytime and you can divide your time between the beach and eating on the seafront, a major occupation here.

TAKING A BREAK & AFTER DARK

There's a line of *trattorias* along the seafront, some with outdoor terraces where the fresh fish is displayed in boxes. The queues of

MONDELLO

patrons are long, particularly in summer. Your best bets for take-away food are the waterfront stalls, offering excellent Sicilian dishes such as *pasta con le sarde* (pasta with olive oil and sardines), deep-fried vegetables, shrimps and octopus.

At night, you can bar hop with the young, twenty-something crowd of Palermitani and visitors. Summer nights are lively and fun, as Piazza Mondello is packed with people. Cars with young locals cruise the strip, and music pumps from the open-air discotheques.

Mondello's harbourside – pretty by day and lively by night

OUT OF TOWN

Monreale

Monreale, a small hill town 8 km (5 miles) southwest of Palermo (see map page 112), commands unsurpassed views down the Conca d'Oro (Golden Shell) valley, with the capital in the distance. The town grew up around the Duomo (cathedral) and the royal palace built by the Norman king, William II, in 1174. The life and soul of this old town still radiates around these buildings, surrounded by many tiny streets lined with shops, bars and restaurants.

Tourist information is available from the tourist office in the cathedral square (❶ (091) 656 4501).

GETTING THERE

By road
Monreale is a 20-minute bus ride on either bus 309 or 389, connecting the Piazza dell'Indipendenza in Palermo with the town. The 389 bus drops you right in Piazza Monreale by the Duomo, the 309 leaves you in the centre of town, where it is a few minutes walk along the Corso Pietro Novelli and Via Roma up to the cathedral. If arriving in Monreale by car from Palermo via the Viale Regionale Siciliana, take the Calatafimi-Monreale exit and then follow N186.

SIGHTS & ATTRACTIONS

Duomo (Cathedral)
Legend has it that the vision of the Duomo came to King William in a dream where the Madonna came to him saying that he should build a church with the treasure stolen from the state by his father, William I. She instructed him to make it so grandiose that it would

MONREALE

The Duomo of Monreale was built in 1174 and dedicated to St Mary

rival the splendour of the Palatine Chapel in Palermo, built by his grandfather Roger II. To that endeavour William hired the most skilled craftsmen for the project, sparing no expense.

In 1174, at the young age of 20, William began construction of the cathedral, the Benedictine Abbey, the Archbishop Palace and the Royal Palace. It was his ambition to hand down to posterity his own name and that of his royal Norman house by erecting a magnificent Christian church, a monumental architectural project to be a testimony to his Christian faith. He wanted to

OUT OF TOWN

assume the title of Caliph under the name of '*al-Musta izz bi-llah*' ('He who searches exultation in God'). The king was inspired to his profound religious faith by political and historical reasons of State.

The Latin basilican plan with the Byzantine-type cross plan is not domed and covers a vast area, 102 m (335 ft) long and 40 m (131 ft) wide. It is divided by 18 columns into a nave and aisles with capitals of exquisite workmanship, decorated with mosaic-covered pulvinoes (Byzantine transformation of the Greek abacus), clypei (a shield-like plate, often on the front of an insect's head) of pagan divinities, acanthus leaves and cornucopias overflowing with fruit.

The columns bear Saracen-style pointed arches; the granite floor, with porphyry geometric decorations, is the original one from the 16th century. The walls of the nave, transept and apses are entirely decorated with mosaics on a gilded background, covering a total area of 6,340 sq m (7,582 sq yds).

Although the cathedral is rather plain on the exterior, the glorious interior more than makes up for that. The mosaic decorations are the work of Byzantine and Venetian craftsmen, executed between the end of the 12th century and the beginning of the 13th century, and depict scenes from the Old and New Testaments. All the mosaics in the church were thought to have been completed in just ten years.

In the central apse your eyes are immediately drawn over the wooden ceiling to the mosaic figure of Christ in benediction. The face and shoulders alone are 20 m (66 ft) high, the outstretched arms and hands seem to be encompassing the beauty of the church. Underneath is a stunning mosaic of the Virgin and Child attended to by angels and below this are the saints, each of whom are beautifully coloured and identified by name. Surprisingly included in all this is the figure of Thomas à Becket, marked 'SCS Thomas Cantb'.

MONREALE

He was canonised in 1173 just before the mosaics were begun. It is presumed that William included this as a political show of support for the papacy.

The two side apses are dedicated to Saint Peter (on the right as you enter) and Saint Paul (on the left). The arches before each apse depict the martyrdom of each. The wonderful mosaics in the nave are an animated series that starts with the Creation above the pillars on the right of the altar; the scene continues on through the entire church. The darker aisle mosaics depict the teachings of Jesus, Adam and Eve, Abraham on the verge of sacrificing his son, and Noah's Ark scenes showing the ship being built, animals being loaded aboard and Noah's family peering out of the hatches, as well as the Feeding of the Five Thousand and the Creation itself. There are gloriously simple panels showing God filling the world with animals, water, light and man.

It is difficult to keep your eyes off the mosaics, but be sure to allow time to explore the entire building. Above the two thrones are more mosaics; William receiving the crown from Christ and the king offering the cathedral to the Virgin. Both William I and William II are buried here in the side chapels; the cathedral's benefactor is in the white marble sarcophagus to the right of the apse.

Access to the tower is in the southwest corner of the cathedral, and a climb of the 180 steps will bring you to the roof and magnificent views of the cloisters. If you are not bothered by heights you can walk around the outside of the church and upwards to the central apse.

The cathedral's solid exterior merits a closer look, particularly the triple apse. The delicate polychromatic designs on the limestone and lava rock are quite exquisite. The apse is supported by slender columns and a series of delicate arches. To get the entire effect of

OUT OF TOWN

the enormity and beauty of this you have to circle the cathedral by walking down a street to the left of the entrance.

It is worth visiting the Chiostro dei Benedettini, or, the cloisters, part of William's original Benedictine monastery. The garden is surrounded by 216 twin columns supporting pointed arches,

MONREALE

a legacy of the Arab influence in Sicilian art. The carved capitals of the 12th-century columns depict various scenes; armed hunters doing battle with beasts, men lifting a casket of wine, and on others

◐ *The impressive cloisters at Monreale cathedral*

OUT OF TOWN

are flowers, birds, snakes and foliage. Enter the cloisters from Piazza Gugliemo, in the corner by the right-hand tower of the cathedral.

Once back inside you can purchase tickets for the collection of the reliquaries in the treasury at the end of the left aisle. ● 08.00–18.30 May–Oct; 08.00–12.30, 15.30–18.30 Nov–Apr. Admission charge

Instituto Statale d'Arte per il Mosaico

If you are interested in watching mosaic restorers at work, the Instituto Statale d'Arte per il Mosaico near the Carabenieri barracks will keep you occupied for hours. ⓐ Via Biagio Giordano 14 ❶ (091) 640 4450 ● 08.00–17.00 Mon–Fri, 08.00–14.00 Sat, closed Sun ⓝ Bus: 389

TAKING A BREAK

There's a good selection of places to eat in the streets just off the Piazza Duomo, though they can be pricey.

Mizzica £–££ If you walk up towards the Duomo and head left down a street before reaching the apse you will come to Mizzica, a popular choice with tourists. ⓐ Via Cappuccini 6 ❶ (091) 640 8643 ● 12.30–15.30, 19.30–23.00 Wed–Mon, closed Tues ⓝ Bus: 389

Trattoria da Peppino £–££ Family-run *trattoria* offering decent meals and great pizzas. ⓐ Via B Civiletti 12 ❶ (091) 640 7770 ● 12.30–15.30, 19.30–23.00 Wed–Mon, closed Tues ⓝ Bus: 305, 309, 389

Bricco & Bacco ££ Standard brasserie-cum-wine bar offering an inexpensive menu. ⓐ Via B D'Acquisto 13 ❶ (091) 641 7773 ● 12.30–15.30, 19.30–23.00 Tues–Sun, closed Mon ⓝ Bus: 389

TRADITIONAL ENTERTAINMENT

Monreale provides a beautiful environment in which to enjoy some unique local entertainment. **Sanicola Theatre** (Via Benedetto 33 (091) 640 9441) offers puppet shows on summer evenings. This is far from being end of the pier stuff (indeed it's folk culture, no less), and many of the playlets performed have been passed down since medieval times.

The Festival of Sacred Music (Settimana de Musica Sacra), which takes place between September and December, is a series concerts of sacred, spiritual and liturgical music held in the town's churches. The aesthetic heights reached in these modest events can be breathtaking. For information contact the tourist office. Via N Nasi 27 (091) 639 8011

ACCOMMODATION

There is limited accommodation in town. The following two options are recommended and will not break your budget.

Carrubella Park £–££ Pleasant, family-run inn, close to everything. Via Umberto 1 (091) 640 2187

La Ciambra Bed & Breakfast £–££ Wedged into a web of narrow streets behind the Duomo's apse. Bright, clean, good value for money. Via Sanches 23 (091) 640 9565 www.laciambra.com

OUT OF TOWN

Trapani & Marsala

Trapani (see map, page 112) is the first of three major towns on Sicily's western edge (Erice and Marsala being the other two). Although it is mostly modern, Trapani's old centre – on a narrow arm of land pointing out into the sea – is elegant. The town's rather plain monuments give no hint as to its long and impressive history.

Trapani has been known as the salt capital of Italy since the days when it was under Phoenician control. It was the Phoenicians who

◐ *The north side of Trapani – Lungomare Dante Alighieri*

TRAPANI & MARSALA

built the original basins and windmills to collect the salt, which they then exported all over the Mediterranean. The Normans continued the industry, and the salt is still being extracted today, although the methods used and the efforts expended have changed as processes have become mechanised. The picturesque windmills lining the roads are still used to pump seawater from one basin to the other. And even though automation has come to the region, you can see bare-chested men toiling with shovels and carting full wheelbarrows across the pans to a conveyor belt which dumps 2 m- (6-and-a-half ft-) high mounds of white salt along the banks of the saltpans.

OUT OF TOWN

To get out and explore the surrounding area, it would be best to hire a car. In Nubia, approximately 6 km (4 miles) south in the direction of Marsala on the Provincial Road SP 21, is a site that reflects Trapani's history in the salt industry, the **Riserva Naturale Salina de Trapani e Paceco** (❷ Via Garibaldi ❶ (092) 386 7700 ❿ www.salineditrapani.it), a saltwater nature reserve habitat where 170 species of birds, both resident and migratory, have been recorded. The road skirts around the edge of a lagoon and provides fine views of the local salt works, panels of shimmering water strategically laid out and separated by thin strips of earth.

Marsala is an excellent day or overnight trip. Besides being world famous for its wine (see page 139), the town has an interesting history. The Carthaginians founded it on Cape Lilibeo (now called Cape Boeo) in 396 BC after fleeing nearby Motya, which had been destroyed by armies of Syracusans, and named it Lilybaeum. It fell to the Romans in 241 BC and saw the arrival of Julius Caesar in 47 BC when he was en route to North Africa. It was while the town was under the rule of the Saracens that the name was changed to Marsa el Allah, meaning port of God.

GETTING THERE

By rail

Trapani is approximately 100 km (62 miles) southwest of Palermo, reachable by train in a time of two hours. The train station is located in Piazza Umberto I. For further information and timetables, contact the **FS** train network on ❿ www.trenitalia.it

Marsala is 31 km (19 miles) south of Trapani, 124 km (77 miles) southwest of Palermo. Its rail station is at the southeastern edge of town on Via A Fazio, a 15-minute walk from the centre.

TRAPANI & MARSALA

By road

Trapani is about three hours away from Palermo by bus, and the bus station is also located in Piazza Umberto I. For further information and timetables, contact **Autoservizi Segesta Bus** (🛈 (092) 321 754). For Marsala, buses arrive centrally at Piazza del Popolo (also known as Piazza Marconi) near Porto Garibaldi.

TRAPANI

Trapani, the ancient Drepanon (sickle), extends along a curving piece of land that ends in two tentacles jutting into the sea; one is occupied by the Torre di Ligny, built in 1671 as a defensive bastion, the other by a *lazaretto*, a house used for the treatment of lepers.

Legend has it that the coastline was formed by the sickle that was dropped by the goddess of agriculture, Demeter (Ceres), while she desperately sought her daughter Persephone, who had been carried off by Hades. The northern edge of the coastline provides protected anchorages and moorings for fishing boats. The well-protected harbour handles large consignments of salt gathered in the salt pans just south of the town and tuna fish processed at the local canning factory. Each morning on the shore opposite the harbour a lively and boisterous fish market is held.

Trapani profited by its position looking out towards Africa. It was a stopover on sea routes linking Tunis, Naples, Anjou and Aragon, a role it played throughout the Middle Ages, when European royalty passed each other on the quayside. The Navarrese king Theobald died here in 1270; in 1272 Edward I of England landed here after a crusade to learn that he had inherited the throne. Peter of Aragon arrived in 1282 to claim the Sicilian throne after the expulsion of the Angevin French.

OUT OF TOWN

The most exciting time to visit is over Easter when the old town is thronged with crowds of people participating in the processions and festivities of Holy Week. The celebrations culminate on Good Friday with the Processione dei Misteri, when 20 groups of sculpted figures, dating back to 1650, are borne through the streets all day and night by, as Sicilian tradition mandates, men from various church associations.
Trapani Tourist Office a Piazzetta Saturno (092) 329 000

SIGHTS & ATTRACTIONS

Almost everything of interest in Trapani is found in the old town, which is about a 15-minute walk west from the train station. Although there has been some restoration of churches and palaces over the years, off the main corso and away from the central shopping areas there is a derelict and scruffy look to the city, with litter-covered streets and *palazzi* allowed to crumble from years of accumulated grime.

You will not see any of this if you stick to the Via Vittorio Emanuele, the old town's pedestrianised main street that is dominated at its eastern end by the pink marble front of the Palazzo Senatorio, the 17th-century town hall. With its twin clocks separated by an elegant eagle, the building adds a bit of grandeur to the thin promenading strip hemmed in by balconied *palazzi* and some baroque churches, the best of which is the Cattedrale San Lorenzo.

Biblioteca Fardelliana

Located near the church of Sant'Angelo, this small museum has engravings from the Gatto collection, including views of the Trapani area from the 17th to 20th centuries. (092) 321 506 09.00–13.30 July & Sept; 10.00–13.00 Aug; 09.00–13.30, 15.00–19.30 Mon–Fri, 09.00–13.30 Sat, closed Sun, Oct–June

Cattedrale San Lorenzo
This 17th-century cathedral is dedicated to Saint Lawrence. Its fabulous baroque exterior porticos and cupolas, along with the gigantic interior, have been restored in recent years to their original sandy hue. Inside is a *Crucifixion* attributed to Van Dyke.
ⓐ Via Vittorio Emanuele ⓣ (092) 323 362 ⓞ 09.00–12.00, 17.00–18.00 Mon–Fri, 09.00–12.00 Sat, Sun & public holidays
ⓘ Donations welcome

Centro Storico
The medieval district of the old town is situated on the headland pointing out to sea. The tip was developed by the Spanish in the 14th century (Quartiere Palazzo), and remodelled in the baroque style several centuries later. The oldest section was built in true Moorish fashion around a tight network of interconnecting narrow streets that originally would have been enclosed by walls.

Museo Regionale Pepoli
Adjacent to the Santuario dell'Annunziata, the museum is housed in the former Carmelite convent. In a sumptuous setting there is a wide collection of archaeological finds, sculpture and Sicilian paintings from the 12th through to the 18th centuries, and a large collection of Trapani art that includes coral carvings and jewellery. The most important works are the pieces of Gagini statuary, a bronze horse and rider by Giacomo Serpotta, a 16th-century marble doorway by Berrettaro Bartolomeu, a *Pieta* by Roberto Oderisio and an 18th-century majolica-tiled scene, *La Mattanza* (tuna slaughter), with the fishermen depicted corralling and hauling the fish into their boat. ⓐ Via Conte Agostino Pepoli 200, the main entrance is through the Villa Pepoli ⓣ (092) 355 3269

OUT OF TOWN

🕐 09.00–13.30 Tues–Sun, closed Mon, 09.00–12.30 festivals and holidays

Museo del Sale di Nubia (Salt Museum of Nubia)
This small, interesting salt museum has been set up in a 300-year-old salt worker's house. It tells and shows the different stages

The importance of the salt industry to this area is readily apparent

TRAPANI & MARSALA

involved in harvesting salt from the saltpans. Among the displays are various special tools used in the extraction and harvest, including mill gearing, windmill vanes, cogwheels, spikes and sprockets. There are photographs of salt workers in action that help to clarify the work involved in the process. ⓐ Via Garibaldi ⓣ (092) 386 7142 ⓒ 09.30–13.00, 15.30–18.30 Mon–Sat, 09.30–13.00 Sun. Thirty-minute guided tours available. Admission charge

OUT OF TOWN

Rua Grande
Constructed in the 13th century, this is Trapani's second main street (Via Vittorio Emanuele was the first); lining it are elegant baroque *palazzi* – at number 86 are the Palazzo Bernardo Ferro and the Sede del Vescovado (Bishop's Palace).

Rua Nova
Now called Via Garibaldi, the Aragonese laid the 'new road' in the 13th century. In the 18th century aristocrats built their *palazzi* and churches along it; Palazzo Riccio di Morana, Palazzo Milo and Badia Nuova (Santa Maria del Soccorso), whose interior is highly decorated with baroque polychrome marble and contains several elaborate galleries. ❸ Badia Nuova ❶ 08.15–13.00 ❶ (092) 343 2111

Sant'Agostino
Built by the Knights Templar in the 14th century, the church was heavily damaged during World War II. The beautiful rose window of interlocking stone bands is original. The church is occasionally used as a concert hall; enquire at the tourist office for details on performances. ❸ Piazzetta Saturno, next to the tourist office

Santa Maria di Gesu
The 16th-century church of Santa Maria di Gesu is most interesting. The Catalan doorway displays a diversity characteristic of Trapani – the right-hand one is Gothic, while the other defiantly Renaissance, and there is a good relief in the architrave. Inside, at the end of the nave, is a terracotta *Madonna degli Angeli* designed by Andrea della Robbia that is sheltered beneath a graceful marble canopy carved by

Antonello Gagini. ⓐ Via San Pietro ⓣ (092) 387 2021 ⓒ 07.30–10.00, closed public holidays

Santuario dell'Annunziata

The only reason to go to the modern part of the city is to visit Trapani's most lavishly decorated monument, the Santaurio dell'Annunziata, a 14th-century Carmelite convent and church whose cloisters hold the town's main museum. The church was built in the 14th century and was enlarged in 1760 and, unfortunately, only the façade, with its Gothic portal and rose-coloured window, is original.

The interior holds several magnificent chapels, two of which are dedicated to Trapani's fishermen and seamen. One chapel carries the façade's shell motif design around the entire wall space.

Extending from behind the main altar of the chapel is the magnificent Cappella della Madonna; entrance is gained through a Renaissance arch designed in the 16th century by the Gagini family. The delicate bronze gates date back to 1591. On the altar is Trapani's sacred idol, the statue of a smiling *Madonna and Child*, attributed to Nino Pisano in the 14th century. Over the Madonna is an ostentatious marble canopy sculpted by Antonino Gagini. It is surrounded by polychrome marble. ⓐ Via Conte Agostino Pepoli 178 ⓣ (092) 353 9184 ⓒ 07.00–12.00, 16.00–18.00 ⓢ Bus: 24, 25, 30 from Piazza Vittorio Emanuele and get off at the park, Villa Pepoli, which is in front of the building

Via Torrearsa

Back at the eastern end of the Via Vittorio Emanuele, Via Torrearsa is one of the old town's main shopping streets. At the northern end is an excellent daily morning market in the Piazza Mercato di Pesce;

OUT OF TOWN

fish, fruit, vegetables, breads, local tuna products, olives and cheeses are on sale here, and many can be sampled.

TAKING A BREAK & AFTER DARK

Eating out in Trapani is a very pleasant experience even if most of the restaurants and *trattorias* do not have outdoor seating. What makes it special is the food. Fresh fish and couscous is served almost everywhere, so be sure to try a local pasta speciality – *alla Trapanese* is terrific, being either spaghetti or home-made *busiate* pasta served with a pesto of fresh tomato, basil, garlic and almonds, sometimes accompanied by fried potatoes.

Calvino £ Serves superb hot pizza. Try a local speciality – the *rianata*, made with fresh oregano, tomato, garlic, anchovies and pecorino cheese. ⓐ Via N Nasi 7 ⓣ (092) 321 464 ⓛ 19.00–23.00 Tues–Sun, closed Mon

Ai Lumi ££ A favourite with the locals, this taverna serves regional dishes, such as *ghiotta di pesce* (seafood soup), home-made pasta, grilled meats and fish. ⓐ Via Vittorio Emanuele 75 ⓣ (092) 387 2418 ⓛ 19.00–23.00 Mon–Sat, closed Sun

La Bettolacca ££ Friendly, informal *osteria* known for its excellent risotto, pasta and fish dishes such as oven-baked *bucatini* (like hollow spaghetti) with sardines. ⓐ Via General Enrico Fardella 25, located just off the corso, around the corner from the Messina Hotel ⓣ (092) 321 695 ⓛ 19.00–23.00

P&G £££ A smart restaurant with a great chef who prepares a fantastic *antipasto* selection, excellent grilled fish and *spaghetti*

TRAPANI & MARSALA

alla Trapanese with fried potatoes and served with anchovies, garlic, pine nuts and tomato. ❷ Via Spalti 1 ❶ (092) 354 7701 ❸ 12.00–15.00, 19.00–23.00 Tues–Sun, closed Mon

ACCOMMODATION

Trapani's cheaper accommodation options are all in the Old Town. With the exception of Easter time, finding a place to stay is generally not a problem.

Messina £ Occupying the first floor of the 18th-century Palazzo Bernardo Ferro, it shares the courtyard with Ai Lumi. It is cheap and clean, though bathrooms are shared. Advance reservations suggested. ❷ Via Vittorio Emanuele 71 ❶ (092) 321 198

Ostello per la Gioventu £ The only youth hostel in the area, it is hidden away 3 km (2 miles) out of town and open only after 18.00 (until late) each day. ❷ Contrada Raganzili ❶ (092) 355 2964 ❸ Take bus no. 21 from the station or bus no. 23 from Piazza Vittorio Emanuele, a 15-minute ride and get off at Ospedale Villa dei Gerani; from the stop take the second street on the right and walk 600 m (656 yds) uphill

Maccotta ££ Clean and friendly place behind the Palazzo Senatorio that has spacious modern rooms, the cheapest of which share a bathroom. ❷ Via degli Argentieri 4 ❶ (092) 328 418 or (092) 343 7693

Nuovo Russo ££ Best choice in the old town for comfort and moderate prices. Tile-floored rooms are clean and bright with good bathrooms. Front rooms face the cathedral and have small terraces overlooking the corso. Breakfast and air conditioning available for an extra charge. ❷ Via Tintori 4 ❶ (092) 211 166 or (092) 326 623

Hotel Tiziano £££ Located in the vicinity of the port, this 4-star hotel is neither characteristic nor particularly charming, but clean and with all comforts. Its position and the attentive staff make it a valid option for your stay in Trapani. ⓐ Via G. Rubino 4 ⓣ (092) 322 211 ⓕ (092) 3549 795 ⓦ www.hoteltizianotrapani.com

MARSALA

Marsala scored its place in modern Italian history for its role in the story of the Risorgimento, the struggle for Italian unity in the 19th century. It was from here that Garibaldi started his campaign to drive out the Bourbons, in the company of his red-shirted 'Thousand'. You can see memorials to Garibaldi, the hero of Sicily, in street names and statuary. One of prominence is the Porto Garibaldi, at the end of Via Garibaldi, which recounts the hero's entry into Marsala. Each year on 11 May local enthusiasts in red shirts gather here to re-enact the exploits of Garibaldi's 'Thousand'.

Marsala Tourist Office ⓐ Via XI Maggio 100, off Piazza Repubblica near the Chiesa Madre ⓣ (092) 371 4097

SIGHTS & ATTRACTIONS

The heart of Marsala is Piazza della Repubblica in the town centre, surrounded by a baroque assortment of buildings and narrow traffic-free streets.

Chiesa Madre

This 18th-century church is dedicated to San Tommaso di Canterbury, patron saint of Marsala. In contrast to the elegant baroque exterior, the rather disappointing interior is dark and

gloomy but does hold a number of interesting Gagini sculptures.
ⓐ Piazza della Repubblica ⓛ 08.00–17.00

Insula Romana

Make your way up from Piazza della Repubblica to Via XI Maggio, lined with upmarket shops, pretty courtyards and cafés. At the far end of Via XI Maggio, through the 18th-century Porta Nuova, on the Piazza della Vittoria are the municipal gardens. Beyond the piazza lies Capo Boeo, the westernmost point of Sicily that was the first settlement of the survivors of annihilated Motya. All the town's major antiquities are here, including the old Insula Romana. Housed here is most of what has been excavated so far of the old city of Lilybaeum. Most of it is from the 3rd century BC Roman, as you might guess from the presence of the vomitorium. Lodged in one entire section of the site is the *edificio termale*, or bathhouse. There is some wonderful mosaicwork here; a chained dog at the entrance and a hunting scene in the atrium.

From Piazza della Vittoria, Viale N Sauro leads to the church of San Giovanni, under which is a grotto that is reputed to have been inhabited by the sibyl Lilibetana. There's another slice of mosaic here, and a well whose water is meant to impart second sight.

Museo degli Arazzi

Located behind the *chiesa*, the only display at the *museo* is a collection of eight enormous hand-stitched wool and silk tapestries depicting the capture of Jerusalem. Made in Brussels in the 16th century, they are beautifully turned out in burnished red, gold and green.
ⓐ Via Garraffa 57 ⓛ 09.00–1300, 16.00–18.00 Tues–Sun, closed Mon. Admission charge

OUT OF TOWN

Museo Archeologico

Also behind the church, in one of the stone vaulted warehouses that line the promenade, is the Museo Archeologico, most of whose space is given over to a well preserved exhibit of a warship from the classical period. Displayed in a heat- and humidity-regulated plastic tent, it ranks as the only existing liburnian, a specifically Phoenician or Punic warship. It was probably sunk during the First Punic War in the great sea battle off the Egadi Islands that ended Carthage's rule of the waves. Brought here in 1977 after eight years of underwater surveying by a British team working under the archaeologist Honor Frost, the vessel, originally 35 m (115 ft) long and rowed by 68 oarsmen, has been a fount of information on the period. Throughout the rest of the museum are items found in or around the ship. ⓐ Viale N Sauro (behind the church of San Giovanni) ⓣ (092) 395 2535 ⓞ 09.00–19.00 Tues–Sat, 09.00–13.00 Sun, closed Mon. Admission charge

TAKING A BREAK & AFTER DARK

In the town centre, which empties of life after 21.00, restaurants can be hard to come by. The couple of bars in Piazza della Repubblica are good for a *te freddo alla pesca* (peach tea) and loud discussions about the lottery numbers. To sample some Marsala wine, visit either the **Enoteca Sombrero** (ⓐ Via Garibaldi 32) or one of two adjacent *enoteca*-souvenir shops in Via Lungomare Boeo, by the archaeological museum.

Caffè Millennium £–££ This is the best place in town for breakfast. It offers grilled sandwiches and good coffee, as well as lunch specials (and it stays open late on the weekends). ⓐ Piazza F Pizzo ⓣ (092) 371 1754 ⓞ 08.00–20.00 (closing times vary at the weekend)

A HISTORY OF MARSALA WINE

The Baglio Anselmi, in which Marsala's archaeological museum is housed (see page 138), is one of a number of old *bagli*, or warehouses, that are conspicuous throughout this wine-making region. Many are still used in the making of the famous dessert wine that carries the town's name. It was Englishman John Woodhouse who first exploited the commercial potential of Marsala wine, when he visited the town in 1770. Woodhouse realised that the local wine could travel for long periods without going off when fortified with alcohol. Others followed, including Messers Ingham, Whittaker and Hopps, whose names can still be seen on some of the warehouse doors. (It was the English presence in Marsala that persuaded Garibaldi to launch his campaign here as he judged that the Bourbon fleet would not dare to interfere close to Her Majesty's commercial concerns.)

Marsala owes much of its current prosperity to the marketing of its wine, which is still a thriving industry, though no longer in British hands. You can visit some of the *bagli* and sample the wine for free: try the **Stabilimento Florio**, located on Lungomare Mediterraneo, to the south of town beyond the port (❶ (092) 378 1111) to arrange a guided tour. There is an **Enomuseum** at Contrada Berbaro (3 km/2 miles along the road to Mazara del Vallo), where you can look over the old apparatus used for wine making (❶ (092) 396 9667). Otherwise, you will find Marsala or the sweeter *marsala all'uovo* (mixed with egg yolks) in every bar and restaurant in town.

OUT OF TOWN

Capo Lilybeo £–££ A restored warehouse near the archaeological museum. The food here is terrific – try the *busiate alla Marsigliese* (with shrimp and lobster ragu), and it is also known for its fish couscous (served on Fridays). ⓐ Via Lungomare Boeo 40 ⓣ (092) 317 2881 ⓛ 12.30–15.00, 19.00–23.00 Tues–Sun, closed Mon

Tratorria Garibaldi £–££ Cosy, upmarket *trattoria* in the centre. Fish is the speciality, though you will eat for less if you choose the grilled meat. ⓐ Piazza Addolorata 5 ⓣ (092) 395 3006 ⓛ 12.30–15.00, 19.00–23.00 Tues–Sun, closed Mon

ACCOMMODATION

Garden £ The cheapest hotel in town has nine rooms and is behind the rail station. Modern and clean. ⓐ Via Gambini 36, right over the train level crossing, then right again ⓣ (092) 398 2320

Villa Favorita £–££ This beautiful, secluded villa is set in its own gardens and has a pool and a charming restaurant. It is 2 km (just over a mile) from the centre and is well signposted. ⓐ Via Favorita 27 ⓣ (092) 398 9100 ⓦ www.villafavorita.com

President £££ Spacious rooms and comfortable beds in this solid business hotel that has a swimming pool. It's a 20-minute walk from the centre. ⓐ Via Nino Bixio 1 ⓣ (092) 399 9333

▶ *The Carabinieri control crime and serve the community*

PRACTICAL
information

PRACTICAL INFORMATION

Directory

GETTING THERE
By air
Budget airlines have made it possible to fly direct from the UK to Palermo easily and cheaply. No frills are offered, but the savings can be quite substantial. Fares depend on what season you choose to travel, the highest being at Easter, anytime between June and mid-August and around Christmas. Prices are considerably lower during September to October, November to March and April to May. For booking flights on-line, four reliable sites are **Expedia** (W www.expedia.co.uk), **Orbitz** (W www.orbitz.com), **Priceline** (W www.priceline.com) and **Travelocity** (W www.travelocity.com).

Airlines in the UK, Ireland and Italy that offer flights are:
Aer Lingus ☏ (UK) 0845 084 4444 W www.aerlingus.ie
Air Berlin ☏ (UK) 0870 738 8880 W www.airberlin.com
Air Malta ☏ (UK) 0845 607 3710 W www.airmalta.com
Alitalia ☏ (UK) 0870 544 8259 W www.alitalia.co.uk
British Airways ☏ (UK) 0870 850 9850 W www.britishairways.com
easyJet ☏ (UK) 0871 750 0100 W www.easyjet.com
Hapag-Lloyd Express ☏ (UK) 0870 606 0519
W www.hapaglloydexpress.com
Meridiana ☏ (UK) (020) 7730 3454 W www.meridiana.it
Ryanair ☏ (UK) 0871 246 0000 W www.ryanair.com
Volare ☏ (UK) 0800 032 0992 W www.volareweb.com

Airlines in the USA and Canada that offer flights are:
Air Canada ☏ 1 888 247 2262 W www.aircanada.ca
American Airlines ☏ 1 800 433 7300 W www.aa.com
British Airways ☏ (USA & Canada) 1 800 AIRWAYS
W www.britishairways.com

DIRECTORY

Delta Airlines ☎ 1 800 221 1212 🌐 www.delta.com
Iberia ☎ 1 800 772 4642 🌐 www.iberia.com
KLM/Northwest ☎ 1 800 447 4747 🌐 www.klm.com
Lufthansa ☎ (USA) 1 800 645 3880; (Canada) 1 800 563 5954
🌐 www.lufthansa.com
SAS Scandinavian Airlines ☎ 1 800 221 2350 🌐 www.flysas.com

Many people are aware that air travel emits CO_2, which contributes to climate change. You may be interested in the possibility of lessening the environmental impact of your flight through the charity Climate Care, which offsets your CO_2 by funding environmental projects around the world. Visit 🌐 www.climatecare.org

By rail

The long train ride south through Italy is a popular way to go (see page 49), allowing stop-offs at various locations before reaching Palermo. The Europe-wide InterRail and Eurail passes give unlimited travel on the FS network. The monthly ***Thomas Cook European Timetable*** has up-to-date schedules for European and Italian services (☎ (UK) 01733 416477; (USA) 1 800 322 3834 🌐 www.thomascookpublishing.com).

Details of rail ticket agencies:

UK and Ireland
Eurostar ☎ 0870 518 6186 🌐 www.eurostar.com
Italian State Railways ☎ (020) 7724 0011 🌐 www.fs-on-line.com
Rail Europe ☎ 0870 584 8848 🌐 www.raileurope.co.uk
Travel Cuts ☎ (020) 7255 1944 🌐 www.travelcuts.co.uk

US and Canada
CIT Rail ☎ (US) 1 800 223 7987 or 1 800 CIT TOUR; (Canada) 1 800 387 0711

PRACTICAL INFORMATION

Ⓦ www.fs-on-line.com and www.cit-tours.com
Europrail International Inc. Ⓣ (Canada) 1 888 667 9734
Ⓦ www.europrail.net
Eurail Ⓣ (US) 1 800 438 7245; (Canada) 1 800 361 7245
Ⓦ www.raileurope.com/us

Australia and New Zealand
CIT World Travel Ⓣ (Australia) 02 9267 1255
Ⓦ www.cittravel.com.au
Rail Plus Ⓣ (Australia) 1300 555 003 or 03 9642 8644;
(New Zealand) 09 303 2484 Ⓦ www.railplus.com.au
Trailfinders Ⓣ (Australia) 1300 780 212 Ⓦ www.trailfinders.com.au

ENTRY FORMALITIES

All that citizens of Britain, Ireland, USA, Canada, New Zealand and Australia need to enter Italy is a valid passport, though they will require a visa if they intend to stay for longer than 90 days. European citizens may stay without a visa for an unlimited period. Citizens of South Africa must have visas to enter Italy, and should check with the embassy in Rome to arrange this. EU citizens are allowed to bring goods for personal use when arriving from another EU country, but should note that they must observe the limits on tobacco (800 cigarettes) and spirits (10 litres over 22 per cent alcohol, 90 litres of wine). Limits for non-EU nationals are 200 cigarettes, one litre of spirits and two litres of wine.

MONEY

Italy's currency is the euro. Notes are issued in denominations of 5, 10, 20, 50, 100, 200, and 500 euros. Coins are issued in denominations of 1, 2, 5, 10, 20, and 50 cents and 1 and 2 euros.

It is a good idea to have some cash on hand when you first arrive. You should be able to order euro notes from your bank, or from branches of Thomas Cook and American Express. You will find ATMs and money exchange bureaux at the airport and around Palermo.

The easiest way not to deal with the exchange is by using your credit or debit card. Before leaving home check with your bank to make sure that your personal identification number gives you access to ATMs/cashpoint machines (*bancomat*) abroad. The cards can be used at hotels, restaurants, some shops and for cash advances. Be aware that in the high season it is not unusual for machines to run out of cash, so keep some in reserve.

It's always a good idea to have some traveller's cheques on hand when you travel. Try to get them in different denominations and keep a record of the cheques' serial numbers in a different place from the actual cheques. On euro traveller's cheques you should not have to pay any commission when exchanging them in Palermo for euros. For other currency cheques there is usually a commission charge of one per cent of the amount changed.

This is never a convenient or cheap experience, but if the need arises for you to have money wired use one of the companies listed below. (It is also possible to have money wired directly from your bank at home to a bank in Palermo. This process takes two business days and there is a charge involved.)

Travellers Express/Moneygram (UK) 0800 6663 9472; (US) 1 800 444 3010; (Canada) 1 800 933 3278; (Australia) 1 800 6663 9472 www.moneygram.com

Western Union (UK) 0800 833 833; (Republic of Ireland) 66 947 5603; (US & Canada) 1 800 CALL CASH; (Australia) 1 800 501 500; (New Zealand) 0800 005 253 www.westernunion.com. Customers in the US and Canada can send money on-line.

PRACTICAL INFORMATION

HEALTH, SAFETY & CRIME

Subjects of the European Union will require an EHIC (European Health Insurance Card) to obtain free medical treatment. In the UK application forms for the EHIC can be obtained in post offices or by applying on-line (W www.ehic.org.uk).

As an EU country Italy has free reciprocal health agreements with other member states, but even if you are covered under this you should make sure you have travel insurance that includes a medical policy. Keep any bills incurred if you will be seeking reimbursement.

In the event that you have anything stolen you must obtain an official statement from the police, not an easy thing to do in Sicily but be persistent as without it you will not be able to claim your loss from the insurance company.

Vaccinations are not required though it is always a good idea to be up to date with tetanus and Hepatitis B shots. The water is safe to drink, but as the taste leaves something to be desired, stay with bottled water, *aqua minerale*, which is inexpensive and readily available. In public fountains be on the lookout for *aqua non potable* signs, which means the water is not safe to drink.

Pharmacists (*farmacia*) are qualified to give you medical advice and dispense prescriptions. Generally one pharmacy stays open all night in each quarter of Palermo. You can locate the name and number of the pharmacy that is open late or all night on any *farmacia* door or listed in the local paper.

If you don't have a spare pair of glasses take a copy of your prescription with you, as an optician, *ottico*, should be able to make you a new pair if yours are lost or damaged.

Petty juvenile crime is rampant in Palermo. Gangs of *scippatori* or bag snatchers strike in crowded streets, marketplaces and parks. Whether on foot or riding scooters they act fast, disappearing before you have had time to react. It is not only handbags they are after, they can whip wallets out of your pocket without your knowing it and tear off visible jewellery and cameras.

Do not flash around large sums of money, leave all jewellery at home, keep a firm grip on cameras, carry your handbag across your body and in front of you, put your wallet in your front pocket, or use a body wallet that you wear either around your waist or your neck under your clothing. Avoid dark streets and alleys. If you find you are out late at night swallow the expense and take a taxi back to your accommodation.

In the event of theft you will need to report it at the Questera, the headquarters of the Polizia Statale. Find the address in the local *Tuttocitta* magazine or ask at your hotel. If you have to deal with the police, be prepared for a lot of frustration and piles of paperwork.

OPENING HOURS

Most shops and businesses are open Monday to Saturday from 09.00 to 13.00 and 16.00 to 20.00. Everything, except bars and restaurants, closes on Sundays. The opening hours of the main banks are 08.30–13.20 and 15.00–16.00 Mon–Fri.

Pharmacies are closed at night, though one in each district remains open late. In August many stores and shops are closed in the afternoons. Some close completely the first two weeks of August.

Except for the Feast of Saint Rosalia on 15 July (see page 10), shops and businesses do not close for religious holidays. Bars and restaurants are open on public holidays; everything else is closed.

Museums are open 09.00–13.00 Tues–Sat, with some open in the afternoons from 16.00–19.00. Archaeological sites are open 09.00–12.00 and 16.00–19.00 Mon–Fri and 09.00–12.00 Sat; summer hours may be longer.

PRACTICAL INFORMATION

Churches are open in the morning from 07.00–12.00 and again in the afternoons from 16.00–19.00. Smaller ones might only be open for early morning and evening services and some open only on Sundays and religious holidays. When visiting a church always dress appropriately.

TOILETS

The signs for women's toilets are *Donne* or *Signore*, while men's facilities will be marked *Uomini* or *Signori*. Public toilets are not easy to find other than at tourist sights and stations, so bars and cafés are the best bet, though you would be expected to buy a drink in these establishments.

CHILDREN

Palermo is a very child-friendly city. Pharmacies and supermarkets carry most baby products, everything from nappies to formula to baby food. Restaurants generally do not offer a children's menu but most will provide a smaller version of an adult meal. Hotels charge extra to put an additional bed in the room. Generous discounts apply to children at most sites and attractions and when travelling on trains.

There is plenty to keep children entertained in Palermo. Kids adore the puppets at Museo Internazionale delle Marionette (International Puppet Museum, see page 100). In summer (July–Sept) free puppet shows are staged here, and puppet shows are also presented at **Teatro Ippogrifo** (⊕ Vicolo Ragusi 4 ⓘ (091) 329 194 ⓑ Bus: 225).

Palermo's public parks offer wonderful interludes for families. Especially inviting is the landscaped oasis of the Orto Botanico (see page 80), offering amenities such as a children's train, play area, bandstands, deer and ducks.

DIRECTORY

It isn't just children who enjoy a performance at the Puppet Theatre

PRACTICAL INFORMATION

The beaches near Palermo are great locations for sun bathing and relaxing

Escape the city and head for a day at the beach at Mondello Lido (see page 110), with its long, sandy beaches, shallow calm waters and plenty of pizza palaces to bring the kids to when they get hungry.

The **Riserva Monte Pellegrino Naturale** (**Monte Pellegrino Nature Reserve** (091) 671 6066 www.riservamontepellegrino.palermo.it) will fascinate the whole family. Monte Pellegrino was occupied as far back as 7000 BC: Palaeolithic incised drawings were found in the Grotto d'Addaura on Pellegrino's northern slopes. Today the mountain is used by picnickers and pilgrims here to visit the shrine of the city's patron saint, St Rosalia. William II's pious niece Rosalia renounced worldly possessions and fled to the mountain in 1159, and nothing was heard from her until the early 17th century, when her bones were discovered on Pellegrino. Pronounced sacred relics, the bones were paraded around the city in a successful attempt to stay the ravages of a terrible plague. The half-hour ride to the mountain is beautiful, offering wide views over Palermo. You enter the **Santuario di Santa Rosalia** (07.00–19.00) through a small chapel, built over a deep cave in the hillside where the bones of Rosalia were discovered

DIRECTORY

in 1624. Inside is a reclining golden statue of the saint. A road to the left of the chapel leads up to the cliff-top promontory, a half-hour's walk, where a statue of St Rosalia stares out over the sprawling city below. Another path, leading up from the Santuario to the right, takes you to the top of the mountain, 600 m (656 yds) high, a 40-minute walk. Other trails that cover the mountain are dotted with families picnicking and children playing.

COMMUNICATIONS
Internet
Internet is increasingly available, both in hotels and at internet cafés around the city. Most hotels now have in-room points or Wi-Fi, or will provide a cable for you to plug into their phone systems. Tourist information offices and kiosks can provide lists of internet cafés and public access points such as libraries, or head to **Aboriginal Internet Cafè** (Via Spinuzza Salvatore 51 (091) 662 2229).

Phone
The telephone service is organised by Telecom Italia. Each office has public booths where the customer pays for units used (*scatti*) at the counter after the call.

Post
The Italian postal service is quite reliable. For letters and postcards you can buy stamps at a *tabacchi* (tobaconist), and for special services you can go to a post office. Post office opening hours are approximately 08.15–13.30 Mon–Fri, and until 12.30 Sat. If you pay extra for *posta priorità* (priority post), your card or letter should arrive the next day in Italy, within three days in the UK and about five days elsewhere.

PRACTICAL INFORMATION

> **TELEPHONING ITALY**
> To call Palermo from abroad, dial 00 (from Europe), 011 (from the US) or 0011 (from Australia), followed by 39 (091) and the local number.
>
> **TELEPHONING ABROAD**
> To make an international call, dial 00, then the country code (UK = 44, Ireland = 353, US and Canada = 1, Australia = 61, New Zealand = 64) and number, omitting the initial zero in UK numbers. Mobile phone numbers begin with 3; if you see an old number with the prefix 03, omit the zero. Your UK, New Zealand and Australian mobile phone will work in Italy; US and Canadian cellphones may not, so be sure to check with your provider before leaving home.

ELECTRICITY

Electrical current in Italy is 220 volts AC and plugs are two pin, round-pronged. British appliances will need a simple adaptor, easily obtained at any electrical or hardware store in Verona or at the airport during your travels. US and other equipment designed for 110 volts will need a transformer (*transformatore di corrente*).

TRAVELLERS WITH DISABILITIES

All of Palermo's major transport terminals have staff and facilities to assist travellers with a disability, so phone ahead to make arrangements. For access to trains, look out for the booklet *I Servizi per la Clientela Disabile* at any rail station, listing the stations with disabled reception centres (*Centro di Accoglienza Disabili*).

In addition, useful organisations for advice and information before your travels include:

RADAR The principal UK forum for people with disabilities.
ⓐ 12 City Forum, 250 City Road, London EC1V 8AF ⓣ (020) 7250 3222 ⓦ www.radar.org.uk

SATH (Society for Accessible Travel & Hospitality) advises US-based travellers with disabilities. ⓐ 347 Fifth Ave, Suite 605, New York, NY 10016 ⓣ (212) 447 7284 ⓦ www.sath.org

TOURIST INFORMATION

Palermo Central Tourist Office ⓐ Piazza Castelnuovo 34
ⓣ (091) 605 8351 ⓦ www.palermotourism.com ⓒ 08.00–14.00, 15.00–18.00 Mon–Fri, 09.00–13.00 Sat, closed Sun

Stazione Centrale Tourist Office ⓐ Piazza Giulio Cesare
ⓣ (091) 616 5914 ⓒ 08.00–20.00 Mon–Fri, 09.00–13.00 Sat, closed Sun

Airport Falcone-Borsellino Tourist Office ⓣ (091) 591 698
ⓒ 08.00–20.00 Mon–Sat, 08.00–14.00 Sun

BACKGROUND READING

The Leopard by Giuseppe Tomasi di Lampedusa. The classic novel about the Sicilian upper class during the 1860s.

Sicily Through Writers' Eyes edited by Horatio Clare. An anthology of writing about Sicily.

Inspector Montalbano by Andrea Camilleri. One of a series of detective novels that really capture the essence of Sicily.

The Honoured Society by Norman Lewis. This history of the mafia in the wake of World War II is essential reading for those interested in the darker side of Sicilian culture.

PRACTICAL INFORMATION

Emergencies

The following are emergency numbers:
Ambulance ❶ 118
Fire brigade ❶ 115
General emergencies ❶ 113
Lost property or theft ❶ 113
Police ❶ 112
Road accident ❶ 116

MEDICAL SERVICES

If you do become ill, need a dentist or are involved in an accident, ask a pharmacist to recommend a doctor or consult the local *Pagine Gialle* (*Yellow Pages*) under Azienda Unita Sanitaria Locale or Unita Sanitaria Locale Pronto Soccorso or phone ❶ 113 and ask for *ospedale* or *ambulanza*. Hospitals in Palermo have English-speaking doctors, but the standards of healthcare are not as high as on mainland Italy.

EMERGENCY PHRASES

Help!	**Fire!**	**Stop!**
Aiuto!	Fuoco!	Fermi!
Ahyootoh!	*Fwohkoh!*	*Fehrmee!*

Call an ambulance/a doctor/the police/the fire service!
Chiami un'ambulanza/un medico/la polizia/i pompieri!
*Kyahmee oon ahmboolahntsa/oon mehdeecoh/
lah pohleetseeyah/ee pohmpyehree!*

EMERGENCIES

If you require emergency treatment, head to the casualty department (*pronto soccorso*) of the hospital (*ospedale*). EU citizens are entitled to free emergency medical treatment if they hold an EHIC (European Health Insurance Card, see page 146).

All pharmacies (*farmacia*) hold lists of those open at night and on Sundays.

POLICE
The civil police force in Palermo that assists tourists is the *polizia*. Should you need to report a theft (*furto*), missing person or any other matter to the police, go to the *questura* (police station). If insurance is involved, ask for a *denuncia*, a stamped form that you must have for filing claims.

Main Police Headquarters Piazza della Vittoria (091) 21 01 11

EMBASSIES & CONSULATES
UK Consulate Via Cavour 117 (091) 326 412
United States Consulate Via Vaccarini 1 (091) 305 857

Other embassies and consulates are located on mainland Italy in Rome, including:
Australian Embassy Via Allessandria 215, Rome (06) 852 721
Canadian Embassy Via Zara 30, Rome (06) 445 5981
Republic of Ireland Embassy Piazza di Campitelli 3, Rome (06) 697 9121
New Zealand Embassy Via Zara 26, Rome (06) 440 2928
South African Embassy Via Tanaro 14, Rome (06) 852 541

INDEX

A
accommodation 34–9
  Marsala 140
  Monreale 123
  Trapani 135–6
air travel 48–9, 142–3
Al Idrisi 96
Albergheria 60–79

B
background reading 153
bars & clubs 30–1
  see nightlife
beach 110–14
Biblioteca
  Fardelliana 128–9
Botanic Garden 80
bus travel 50, 56, 110, 116, 127

C
cafés
  La Kalsa 106–7
  Marsala 138–40
  Monreale 122
  Quattro Canti & Albergheria 76–7
  Via Roma & Vucciria 92–3
Cala, La 99
camping 39
Capo quarter 60–5
Cappella Palatina 73
car hire 58
Catacombe dei Cappuccini 47
Cathedral
  Monreale 116–22
  Palermo 65–6
  Trapani 129
Centro Storico, Trapani 129
Chiesa Madre 136–7
children 148–51
cinemas 31
climate 8

consulates & embassies 155
crime 7, 12–13, 54, 107, 146–7
culture 18–20
currency 144–5
customs regulations 144
cycling 32

D
disabilities 152–3
driving 50–1, 58
Duomo, Monreale 116–22

E
electricity 152
emergencies 156–7
entertainment 30–1
  see also nightlife
events 8–11, 18–20, 45, 123

F
ferries 51
festivals 8–11, 18–20, 45, 98, 123
food & drink 26–9
football 32
Frutta Martorana 62

G
Galleria Regionale di Sicilia 98–100
Gancia, La 100
Giardino Garibaldi 80–2
golf 32
guanat 47

H
health 146, 154–5
Historic Quarter 96–108
history 14–15
hotels
  see accommodation

I
Instituto Statale d'Arte per il Mosaico 122
Insula Romana 137
internet 151

K
Kalsa, La 96–108

L
La Cala 99
La Gancia 100
La Kalsa 96–108
La Magione 102–4
La Martorana 66–7
La Zisa 88
language 25, 29, 48, 157
lifestyle 16–17
listings 20, 31

M
Mafia 7, 12–13
Magione, La 102–4
marina 99
markets 23–5, 62–4, 67, 91, 106
Marsala 126, 136–40
Marsala wine 138–9
Martorana, La 66–7
marzipan 62
Mondello 30, 110–15
money 144–5
Monreale 116–23
Monte Pellegrino Nature Reserve 150
Museo Archeologico Regionale 86–8
Museo Archeologico, Marsala 138
Museo d'Arte e Archeologia 46
Museo degli Arazzi 137
Museo del Risorgimento 88
Museo del Sale di Nubia 130–1
Museo Diocesano 67
Museo Internazionale delle Marionette 100–1
Museo Regionale Pepoli 129–30
music 20

156

INDEX

N
nightlife 30–1
  Mondello 113–4
Nubia 126, 130–1

O
Old Harbour 99
opening hours 27, 147–8
Opera dei Pupi 101–2
Oratorio del Rosario
  di San Domenico 46
Orto Botanico 80

P
Palace of La Zisa 88
Palazzina Cinese 43
Palazzo Aiutamicristo 104
Palazzo Archivescovile 67
Palazzo Chiaramonte 82–3
Palazzo dei Normanni 73–4
Palazzo Mirto 84–5
Palermo Sottosopra 47
Parco de la Favorita 43
parks 33, 43, 45, 80–6, 148
passports & visas 144
pharmacies 146
phones 151–2
Piazza della
  Rivoluzione 104
Piazza delle Poste 89
Piazza Magione 102–4
Piazza Marina 80–3
Piazza Pretoria 67–8
police 147, 155
pollution 6
Porta Nuova 67, 70
post 151
public holidays 11
public transport 56
Puppet Theatre,
  Monreale 123
Puppet Theatre,
  Palermo 101–2

Q
Quattro Canti &
  Alberghería 60–79

R
rail travel 49–50, 126, 143–4
restaurants 26–9
  La Kalsa 108
  Marsala 138–40
  Monreale 122
  Quattro Canti &
    Alberghería 78–9
  Trapani 134–5
  Via Roma & Vucciria 93–4
Riserva Naturale Salina 126
Royal Apartments 74
Rua Grande, Trapani 132
Rua Nova, Trapani 132

S
safety 6–7, 13, 54, 107, 146–7
St John of the Hermits 68
Salt Museum
  of Nubia 130–1
Sanicola Theatre 123
San Cataldo 68
San Domenico 91
San Giovanni
  degli Eremiti 68
San Giuseppe
  dei Teatini 70
Sant'Agostino
  Palermo 64–5
  Trapani 132
Santa Caterina 70
Santa Maria
  degli Angeli 100
Santa Maria
  Dell'Ammiraglio 66–7
Santa Maria dello
  Spasimo 20, 104–5
Santa Maria di Gesu 132–3
Santa Teresa alla Kalsa 105
Sant'Ignazio Martire
  all'Olivella 89–90
Santuario
  dell'Annunziata 133
Santuario di
  Santa Rosalia 150–1

seasons 8
shopping 22–5
  La Kalsa 105–6
  Quattro Canti &
    Alberghería 75–6
  Via Roma &
    Vucciria 91–2
sport 32–3
symbols &
  abbreviations 4

T
taxis 56–8
Teatro Ippogrifo 148
Teatro Massimo 74–5
Teatro Politeama
  Garibaldi 20
tennis 33
theatres 20, 31, 74–5, 148
time difference 48
tipping 28–9
toilets 148
tourist information 20, 153
Trapani 124–36

V
Via Alloro 105
Via Roma 80–95
Via Torrearsa 133–4
Via Vittorio Emanuele 70
Villa Giulia 83–6
Vucciria 86–95

W
weather 8, 46–7
windsurfing 44

Z
Zisa, La 88

WHAT'S IN YOUR GUIDEBOOK

Independent authors Impartial up-to-date information from our travel experts who meticulously source local knowledge.

Experience Thomas Cook's 165 years in the travel industry and guidebook publishing enriches every word with expertise you can trust.

Travel know-how Contributions by thousands of staff around the globe, each one living and breathing travel.

Editors Travel-publishing professionals, pulling everything together to craft a perfect blend of words, pictures, maps and design.

You, the traveller We deliver a practical, no-nonsense approach to information, geared to how you really use it.

SPOTTED YOUR NEXT CITY BREAK?

Then these lightweight CitySpots pocket guides will have you in the know in no time, wherever you're heading. Covering over 80 cities worldwide, they're packed with detail on the most important urban attractions from shopping and sights to non-stop nightlife; knocking spots off chunkier, clunkier versions.

Aarhus	Genoa	Paris
Amsterdam	Glasgow	Prague
Antwerp	Gothenburg	Porto
Athens	Granada	Reykjavik
Bangkok	Hamburg	Riga
Barcelona	Hanover	Rome
Belfast	Helsinki	Rotterdam
Belgrade	Hong Kong	Salzburg
Berlin	Istanbul	Sarajevo
Bilbao	Kiev	Seville
Bologna	Krakow	Singapore
Bordeaux	Kuala Lumpur	Sofia
Bratislava	Leipzig	Stockholm
Bruges	Lille	Strasbourg
Brussels	Lisbon	St Petersburg
Bucharest	Ljubljana	Tallinn
Budapest	London	Tirana
Cairo	Los Angeles	Tokyo
Cape Town	Lyon	Toulouse
Cardiff	Madrid	Turin
Cologne	Marrakech	Valencia
Copenhagen	Marseilles	Venice
Cork	Milan	Verona
Dubai	Monte Carlo	Vienna
Dublin	Moscow	Vilnius
Dubrovnik	Munich	Warsaw
Düsseldorf	Naples	Zagreb
Edinburgh	New York	Zurich
Florence	Nice	
Frankfurt	Oslo	
Gdansk	Palermo	
Geneva	Palma	

Available from all good bookshops, your local Thomas Cook travel store or browse and buy on-line at www.thomascookpublishing.com

Thomas Cook Publishing

ACKNOWLEDGEMENTS & FEEDBACK

Editorial/project management: Lisa Plumridge with Laetitia Clapton
Copy editor: Paul Hines
Layout/DTP: Pat Hinsley & Alison Rayner
Proofreader: Wendy Janes

The publishers would like to thank the following companies and individuals for supplying their copyright photographs for this book:
161 Bar & Restaurant, page 79; Vito Arcomano/Fototeca ENIT, pages 24 & 130–1; Alaman, page 28; Piotr Antoňów/Dreamstime.com, pages 40–1; Archenzo, pages 124–5; Arpingstone, page 141; Giacomo Cutrichio, page 101; Sabrina Dvihally/Dreamstime.com, page 37; Alexandre Fagundes De Fagundes, page 57; Petulia Melideo, pages 103, 109 & 150; Katie Parla, pages 21 & 59; Pasticceria Cappello, page 77; Bernhard J Scheuvens, pages 33, 71, 89 & 117; Peeter Viisimaa/iStockphoto.com, page 9; Caroline Jones, all others.

Send your thoughts to
books@thomascook.com

- **Found a great bar, club, shop or must-see sight that we don't feature?**
- **Like to tip us off about any information that needs a little updating?**
- **Want to tell us what you love about this handy little guidebook and more importantly how we can make it even handier?**

Then here's your chance to tell us all! Send us ideas, discoveries and recommendations today and then look out for your valuable input in the next edition of this title.

Email the above address (stating the title) or write to:
CitySpots Project Editor, Thomas Cook Publishing, PO Box 227, Coningsby Road, Peterborough PE3 8SB, UK.

SPOTTED YOUR NEXT CITY BREAK?

Then these lightweight CitySpots pocket guides will have you in the know in no time, wherever you're heading. Covering over 80 cities worldwide, they're packed with detail on the most important urban attractions from shopping and sights to non-stop nightlife; knocking spots off chunkier, clunkier versions.

Aarhus	Genoa	Paris
Amsterdam	Glasgow	Prague
Antwerp	Gothenburg	Porto
Athens	Granada	Reykjavik
Bangkok	Hamburg	Riga
Barcelona	Hanover	Rome
Belfast	Helsinki	Rotterdam
Belgrade	Hong Kong	Salzburg
Berlin	Istanbul	Sarajevo
Bilbao	Kiev	Seville
Bologna	Krakow	Singapore
Bordeaux	Kuala Lumpur	Sofia
Bratislava	Leipzig	Stockholm
Bruges	Lille	Strasbourg
Brussels	Lisbon	St Petersburg
Bucharest	Ljubljana	Tallinn
Budapest	London	Tirana
Cairo	Los Angeles	Tokyo
Cape Town	Lyon	Toulouse
Cardiff	Madrid	Turin
Cologne	Marrakech	Valencia
Copenhagen	Marseilles	Venice
Cork	Milan	Verona
Dubai	Monte Carlo	Vienna
Dublin	Moscow	Vilnius
Dubrovnik	Munich	Warsaw
Düsseldorf	Naples	Zagreb
Edinburgh	New York	Zurich
Florence	Nice	
Frankfurt	Oslo	
Gdansk	Palermo	
Geneva	Palma	

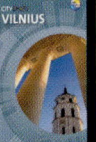

Available from all good bookshops, your local Thomas Cook travel store or browse and buy on-line at www.thomascookpublishing.com

Thomas Cook Publishing

ACKNOWLEDGEMENTS & FEEDBACK

Editorial/project management: Lisa Plumridge with Laetitia Clapton
Copy editor: Paul Hines
Layout/DTP: Pat Hinsley & Alison Rayner
Proofreader: Wendy Janes

The publishers would like to thank the folllowing companies and individuals for supplying their copyright photographs for this book: 161 Bar & Restaurant, page 79; Vito Arcomano/Fototeca ENIT, pages 24 & 130–1; Alaman, page 28; Piotr Antonów/Dreamstime.com, pages 40–1; Archenzo, pages 124–5; Arpingstone, page 141; Giacomo Cuticchio, page 101; Sabrina Dvihally/Dreamstime.com, page 37; Alexandre Fagundes De Fagundes, page 57; Petulia Melideo, pages 103, 109 & 150; Katie Parla, pages 21 & 59; Pasticceria Cappello, page 77; Bernhard J Scheuvens, pages 33, 71, 89 & 117; Peeter Viisimaa/iStockphoto.com, page 9; Caroline Jones, all others.

Send your thoughts to
books@thomascook.com

- **Found a great bar, club, shop or must-see sight that we don't feature?**
- **Like to tip us off about any information that needs a little updating?**
- **Want to tell us what you love about this handy little guidebook and more importantly how we can make it even handier?**

Then here's your chance to tell all! Send us ideas, discoveries and recommendations today and then look out for your valuable input in the next edition of this title.

Email the above address (stating the title) or write to:
CitySpots Project Editor, Thomas Cook Publishing, PO Box 227, Coningsby Road, Peterborough PE3 8SB, UK.